THE COMPLETE LOG4J MANUAL

Ceki Gülcü

This manual applies to log4j version 1.2 and later.

The complete log4j manual
by Ceki Gülcü

FIRST EDITION   February 2003
REPRINTED   August 2003

PUBLISHED BY   QOS.ch

ISBN 2-9700369-0-8

Printed and bound in Montreux, Switzerland

To my grandfather Leon Y. Bahar,
whose determination and resilience
resonate like a beacon.

TABLE OF CONTENTS

FOREWORD

I have supported production systems for several years now and written my own logging frameworks to provide the ability to access fine grained information on demand, as this is critical in a production system.

In my experience it is virtually impossible to adequately replicate usage patterns and data that arise in production environments in QA/test environments. Invariably this means having to debug a running production system and debuggers, while great tools (I have attached to a production C++ system and dumped out the assembly code to figure out why a process was stalled), often cannot be used in production because they may not available, and can be too intrusive to use. For example, trying to catch a threading problem in a debugger can be next to impossible if it involves a subtle race/timing condition.

Therefore, the ability to diagnose problems with a fine grained on demand logging framework has always been a great tool for me. One of my first tasks on joining the JBoss project was to move from an existing proprietary logging framework to Log4j to bring our logging framework up to snuff with the rest of the technology. We have customized loggers, appenders, levels, and layouts with virtually no trouble.

Having read the complete log4j manual I have created a `RepositorySelector` for use in my JBoss Administration and Development book to allow for the selection of chapter and even example specific logging configuration file selection in a very simple fashion. I am also creating JBoss application server `RepositorySelector` that will allow individual component deployments to install their own Log4j configuration rather than having to modify the server configuration, or rely on class loader scoping tricks.

I'm sure you will find the book as useful as I have.

—SCOTT STARK, Chief Technology Officer, JBoss Group, LLC

PREFACE

> Writing a book is a little more difficult than writing a technical paper, but writing software is a lot more difficult than writing a book.
>
> —DONALD KNUTH, *"All Questions Answered,"* October 5, 2001

Have you ever witnessed a system failure and spent hours trying to reproduce it? Infrequently occurring bugs are treacherous and cost tremendously in terms of time, money and morale. With enough contextual information, most[1] bugs take only minutes to fix. Identifying the bug is the hard part.

Ideally, a well-thought out battery of test cases will catch bugs early in the development cycle. However, it is plainly impossible to test everything no matter how much work you put into it, in all but select few, usually very small applications. Logging equips the developer with *detailed context* on application failures. On the other hand, testing provides quality assurance and confidence in the application. Logging and testing should not be confused. The two are complementary. The larger your application the more testing and the more logging you will need to do. Just testing will not suffice; just logging will certainly not. When logging is wisely used, it can prove to be an essential tool.

Contents of this Book

This manual describes the log4j API in considerable detail, including its features and design rationale. It is intended for developers already familiar with the Java language but new to log4j, as much as for experienced log4j users. With the aid of introductory material and the examples, new users should quickly come up to speed. Seasoned log4j users will also find fresh material not discussed anywhere else. Advanced topics are also covered in detail so that the reader can harness the full power of log4j.

Chapter 1 gives a gentle introduction to log4j. Chapter 2 introduces the basic log4j concepts as well as the overall log4j architecture. Configuration scripts, first in properties format and then XML format, are presented in Chapter 3. These first three chapters cover the basic features of log4j. Chapters 4, 5, and 6 discuss log4j

---

[1] Most bugs are shallow only a rare few require architectural changes.

components, namely appenders, layouts and filters in considerable depth. Advanced topics such as diagnostic contexts and extension techniques are deferred to later chapters.

The reader is highly encouraged to frequently consult the log4j javadoc documentation shipped with log4j. This documentation is also available online at:

  http://jakarta.apache.org/log4j/docs/api/index.html.

Conventions Used In This Book

Italics is used for:

- Pathnames, filenames, and application names

- New terms, usually where they are defined

- Internet addresses, such as email addresses, domain names and URLs

Bold is used for:

- Extra emphasis, especially in configuration files.

`Constant Width` is used for:

- All Java code listings

- Command lines and options that should be typed verbatim on the screen

- Tag names in XML configuration scripts

- Anything that appears literally in a Java program, including constants, class names, interface names, method names, and variables.

`Constant Width Italic` is used for:

- Replaceable elements in configuration files

- Attribute names in a XML configuration file

`Constant Width Bold` is used for:

- System properties

Tunga is used for:

Properties or options of log4j components (e.g. appenders)

Comments and Questions

Although I have tried my best, this book undoubtedly contains omissions, inaccuracies and mistakes. You can help me improve it by sending your suggestions to

ceki@apache.org or alternatively to *log4j-user@jakarta.apache.org*

The latter is an open mailing list dedicated to log4j. Reporting errors, typos, misleading or unclear statements is highly appreciated. In case you have a hard time finding certain information contained in the manual, you are encouraged to share your experiences. This will improve the index, helping you as well as other readers.

As log4j continues to grow and improve, so will this manual. Future editions will strive to track and document important new log4j features. By buying this manual, you are not only acquiring the most complete log4j documentation but also sustaining the log4j development effort. *Thank you.*

Acknowledgments

My gratitude goes to Dr. N. Asokan for reviewing an earlier manuscript of this manual. He is also one of the originators of the hierarchical logger concept along with Dr. Michael Steiner. I am indebted to Nelson Minar, of JXTA fame, for encouraging me to write the short log4j manual that in time became this book. Many readers have reported errors helping to improve the quality of this book. I thank them sincerely.

The quality of the project benefited tremendously from a less known Jakarta project called Gump (*http://jakarta.apache.org/gump*). When the `Logger` class was first introduced, it was a super-class of `Category`. This caused a rather subtle and unpredictable incompatibility bug that was detected by Gump in about 24 hours. Nicholas Wolff later suggested a far more reliable migration strategy. Without Gump, it would have taken us weeks or even months to detect the problem, at which time it would have been too late to fix it. In short, without Gump, log4j could not possibly offer the same guarantees of backward compatibility. Life is like a box of chocolates, you never know what you are going to get.

Log4j is the result of a collective effort. My special thanks go to all the authors who have contributed to the project. Without exception, the best features in the package have all originated in the log4j community. Log4j became publicly available in April 1999. Something amazing and unique happened shortly afterwards: patches started to make their appearance. Comments and code began flowing in from all corners of the world. I can hardly describe the exhilaration felt when receiving an ingenious patch, especially if it arrives just a few hours after a new release.

The contributors to the log4j project are too numerous to fully list here. However, contributions from fellow developers, Oliver Burn, James P. Cakalic, Paul Glezen, Anders Kristensen, Jon Skeet, Kevin Steppe, Chris Taylor and Mark Womack stand out particularly. I could not thank them enough. I am grateful to Costin Manolache of Tomcat fame for allowing me to include some of his code.

Log4j owes its success to its active user base. In fact, the contents of this manual itself were mostly inspired from questions and comments asked on the log4j mailing lists. Hopefully, many of those questions will be answered in this manual.

1

INTRODUCTION

The morale effects are startling. Enthusiasm jumps when there is a running system, even a simple one. Efforts redouble when the first picture from a new graphics software system appears on the screen, even if it is only a rectangle. One always has, at every stage in the process, a working system. I find that teams can grow *much more complex entities in four months than they can* build.
> —FREDERIC P. BROOKS, JR., *The Mythical Man-Month*

Almost every large application includes its own logging or tracing API. In compliance with this rule, the E.U. SEMPER project decided to write its own tracing API. This was in early 1996. After countless enhancements, several incarnations and much work that API evolved to become log4j, a popular logging package for Java. The package is distributed under the Apache Software License[2], a full-fledged open source license certified by the open source initiative (*http://www.opensource.org*). The latest log4j version, including full-source code, class files and documentation can be found at

> *http://jakarta.apache.org/log4j*

Log4j has been ported by independent authors to C, C++, Qt/C++, Eiffel, Lotus Script, Oracle PL/SQL, Perl, PHP, Python, Ruby and the much maligned C#.

Inserting log statements into code is a low-tech debugging method. It may also be the only way because debuggers are not always available or applicable. This is usually the case for multithreaded applications and distributed applications at large. Experience indicates that logging acts as an important component in the development cycle. It offers several advantages. It can provide precise context about an execution of the application. Once inserted into the code, the generation of logging

---

[2] A copy of the Apache Software License is included at the end of this book.

output is automatic. Moreover, log output can be made persistent so it can be studied later. In addition to its use in the development cycle, a sufficiently rich logging package can also be viewed as an auditing tool.

As Brian W. Kernighan and Rob Pike put it in their excellent book "The Practice of Programming"

> As personal choice, we tend not to use debuggers beyond getting a stack trace or the value of a variable or two. One reason is that it is easy to get lost in details of complicated data structures and control flow; we find stepping through a program less productive than thinking harder and adding output statements and self-checking code at critical places. Clicking over statements takes longer than scanning the output of judiciously placed displays. It takes less time to decide where to put print statements than to single-step to the critical section of code, even assuming we know where that is. More important, debugging statements stay with the program; debugging sessions are transient.

Logging does have its drawbacks. It can slow down an application. If too verbose, it can cause scrolling blindness. To alleviate these concerns, log4j is designed to be fast and flexible. Since logging is rarely the main focus of an application, log4j API strives to be simple to understand and use.

Installing

The latest version of log4j can be downloaded from

> *http://jakarta.apache.org/log4j/docs/download.html*

Releases are available in two formats: *zip* and *tar.gz*. After unpacking the distribution, you should see the file *LOG4J_HOME/dist/lib/log4j-VERSION.jar* where LOG4J_HOME is the directory where you unpacked the log4j distribution and VERSION is the version of the log4j distribution you downloaded. To start using log4j simply add this jar file to your CLASSPATH.

Running the Examples

This book contains many examples to facilitate hands-on experience. The source code for the examples can be obtained electronically at:

> https://www.qos.ch/shop/products/clm/log4jManual.zip

Assuming you unpack this file under the *LOG4J_MANUAL/* directory, you will find the source code under *LOG4J_MANUAL/examples/*. As a convenience, compiled classes are available under the *LOG4J_MANUAL/examples/classes/* directory. In order to compile or execute the examples you must have the *log4j-VERSION.jar* as well as the *LOG4J_MANUAL/examples/classes* directory in your CLASSPATH. Note that some examples using the DOMConfigurator require the presence of a JAXP compatible parser.

If you wish to compile the examples, change the current directory to *LOG4J_MANUAL/examples/* and invoke a recent version of Apache Ant, as appropriate for your environment. Note that apart from Apache Ant, all required libraries are included under the *LOG4J_MANUAL/lib/* directory.

First Baby Step

After you have added *log4j-VERSION.jar* and *LOG4J_MANUAL/examples/classes* to your CLASSPATH, you can test a small program that uses log4j.

```
package chapter1;
import org.apache.log4j.Logger;

public class HelloWorld1 {
  static Logger logger = Logger.getLogger("chapter1.HelloWorld1");

  static public void main(String[] args) {
    logger.debug("Hello world.");
  }
}
```

HelloWorld1 class is defined to be in the chapter1 package. It starts by importing the org.apache.log4j.Logger class. It also defines a static final variable, logger, of type Logger. The logger variable is initialized to the value returned by Logger.getLogger("chapter1.HelloWorld1"). I will shortly explain what loggers are and the reasons for the "chapter1.HelloWorld1" string parameter. For the time being, I request your patience.

Within the main method, we invoke the debug method of the logger object with the string "Hello World.". Put differently, the main method contains a single logging statement of level debug containing the message "Hello World.".

You may wish to compile the file *examples/chapter1/HelloWorld1.java*. Note that as a convenience, class files are already included in the *log4jManual.zip* file mentioned earlier.

Try to run *HelloWorld1* as follows:

```
java chapter1.HelloWorld1
```

This will not produce any logging output but instead the following warning.

```
log4j:WARN No appenders could be found for logger (chapter1.HelloWorld1).
log4j:WARN Please initialize the log4j system properly.
```

Log4j is complaining because we have not configured it just yet. There are many different ways for configuring log4j as you shall discover in Chapter 3. The simplest (and least flexible) way is by calling the `BasicConfigurator.configure` method. Here is our second and more successful attempt.

```
package chapter1;
import org.apache.log4j.Logger;
import org.apache.log4j.BasicConfigurator;

public class HelloWorld2 {
  static Logger logger = Logger.getLogger("chapter1.HelloWorld2");

  static public void main(String[] args) {
    BasicConfigurator.configure();
    logger.debug("Hello world.");
  }
}
```

Running this example will produce the following output on the console.

```
10 [main] DEBUG chapter1.HelloWorld2  - Hello world.
```

The output contains relative time, that is, the number of milliseconds that elapsed since the start of the program until the invocation of the logging request[3], the name of the invoking thread between brackets, the level of the request, the logger name, and finally the message. As you can see, incorporating log4j into your application is rather easy. The required steps remain essentially the same, even in large applications.

---

[3] More precisely, relative time is the elapsed time in milliseconds since loading of the `LoggingEvent` class by the JVM until the invocation of the logging request The `LoggingEvent` class is loaded into memory when the first logging request is made. Thus, the relative time of the first logging message is usually zero although it can also be a small positive integer.

Recipe for using log4j in your applications

Here are the steps one usually takes in order to use log4j in one's applications.

1. Configure log4j for your environment. Log4j offers many sophisticated means of configuration, `BasicConfigurator.configure()` being the simplest but also the least flexible. Chapter 3 is dedicated to the topic of log4j configuration.

 Log4j normally needs to be configured only once. Some new users try to configure log4j in each and every class. This is very inefficient and just plain wrong.

---

2. In every class where you wish to perform logging, retrieve a `Logger` object by invoking the `Logger.getLogger` method and passing it a `String`, commonly the fully qualified name of the containing class. This logger object is usually declared as static final.

   There is a variant of the `Logger.getLogger` method that takes a `Class` object as argument instead of a `String`. It is intended as a syntactic sugar. For some class `X` in package `com.wombat`, the following three expressions are equivalent:

   ```
   Logger.getLogger("com.wombat.X");  // String variant
   Logger.getLogger(X.class.getName()); // another String variant
   Logger.getLogger(X.class);  // convenient Class variant
   ```

3. Use this logger instance by invoking its printing methods, namely the `debug()`, `info()`, `warn()`, `error()` and `fatal()` methods or the more generic `log()` method. This will produce logging output on selected devices.

Before delving into the details of log4j's architecture in the next chapter, it is a good idea for the reader to try out the examples in this introductory chapter. As Fredic O. Brooks observes in this classical work *"The Mythical Man-Month"*, donning a belt of success, however modest, has extraordinarily positive effects on spirits.

Building log4j

Like most Java applications today, log4j relies on Apache Ant as its build tool. Ant is available from *http://ant.apache.org/*. Ant requires a build file named *build.xml* which already ships with log4j distributions. Required components from other projects are specified in the *build.properties* file, an example of which is supplied in the *build.properties.sample* file.

Building *all* log4j components requires several external libraries. For instance, the SMTPAppender relies on the JavaMail API version 1.2, in turn; the JavaMail API requires the JavaBeans Activation Framework package. The JMSAppender requires the JMS API as well as JNDI. The JMS API is usually bundled with JMS-compatible middleware products. The DOMConfigurator is based on the JAXP API. Given that a JAXP-compatible XML parser is required to run Ant build files, you need not worry about setting the parser when building log4j; Ant will do it for you. Building the org.apache.log4j.jmx package requires the JMX interface API.

Fortunately, all these APIs are optional. If one of the APIs is unavailable, then log4j will only build the components that it can build successfully. Thus, running "ant build" out of the box will build most components except the SMTPAppender, JMSAppender and the org.apache.log4j.jmx package.

Log4j distributions contain complete source code such that you can modify parts of log4j library and build your own version of it. You may even redistribute the modified version, as long as you adhere to the conditions of the Apache Software License. In particular you may *not* call the modified version "log4j" or claim that it is endorsed by the Apache Software Foundation. The Apache Software License is reproduced verbatim and then discussed in the appendixes (on page 198).

2

LOG4J ARCHITECTURE

All true classification is genealogical.

—CHARLES DARWIN, *The Origin of Species*

It is difficult, if not impossible, for anyone to learn a subject purely by reading about it, without applying the information to specific problems and thereby forcing himself to think about what has been read. Furthermore, we all learn best the things that we have discovered ourselves.

—DONALD KNUTH, *The Art of Computer Programming*

The previous chapter presented a very simple usage case for log4j. This chapter discusses the log4j architecture and the rules governing its components. Log4j has three main components: *loggers*, *appenders* and *layouts*. These three types of components work together to enable developers to log messages according to their level. They control the format of log messages as well as their output destination.

The reader familiar with the `java.util.logging` API introduced in JDK 1.4, will recognize that log4j's architecture is very similar though log4j offers much richer functionality. Log4j requires JDK 1.1 whereas `java.util.logging` will only run on JDK 1.4. Most of the concepts outlined in this document are reproduced with little variation in `java.util.logging` albeit with somewhat different names. In case you had any doubts regarding log4j's lineage, the present log4j architecture dates back to early 1999, the JDK 1.4 logging API was not even a proposal at the time.

Logger hierarchy

The first and foremost advantage of any logging API over plain `System.out.println` statements resides in its ability to disable certain log statements while allowing others to print unhindered. This capability assumes that the logging space, that is, the space of all possible logging statements, is categorized according to some developer-chosen criteria.

This observation had previously led us to choose category as the central concept of the package. However, since log4j version 1.2, `Logger` class has replaced the `Category` class. For those familiar with earlier versions of log4j, the `Logger` class can be considered as a mere alias to the `Category` class.

Loggers are named entities. Logger names are case-sensitive and follow the Named Hierarchy Rule:

Named Hierarchy Rule

> A logger is said to be an ancestor of another logger if its name followed by a dot is a prefix of the descendant logger name. A logger which is an immediate ancestor of a descendant is said to be a parent logger. The immediate descendant is said to be a child logger.

For example, the logger named "org.gopher" is a parent of the logger named "org.gopher.Tail". Similarly, "java" is a parent of "java.util" and an ancestor of "java.util.Vector". This naming scheme should be familiar to most developers.

The root logger resides at the top of the logger hierarchy. It is exceptional in three ways:

- it always exists,

- its level cannot be set to null,

- it cannot be retrieved by name.

Invoking the class static `Logger.getRootLogger` method retrieves it. All other loggers are instantiated and retrieved with the class static `Logger.getLogger` method. This method takes the name of the desired logger as a parameter. Some of the most frequently used methods of the `Logger` class are listed below.

```
package org.apache.log4j;

public class Logger {

  // Logger creation & retrieval methods:
  public static Logger getRootLogger();
  public static Logger getLogger(String name);

  // printing methods:
  public void debug(Object message);
  public void info(Object message);
  public void warn(Object message);
  public void error(Object message);
  public void fatal(Object message);

  // printing methods for exceptions:
  public void debug(Object message, Throwable t);
  public void info(Object message, Throwable t);
  public void warn(Object message, Throwable t);
  public void error(Object message, Throwable t);
  public void fatal(Object message, Throwable t);

  // generic printing method:
  public void log(Level p, Object message);
}
```

Logger creation and retrieval

Each and every logger is tightly bound to the hierarchy that creates it. As mentioned previously, all non-root loggers are instantiated and retrieved with the class static `Logger.getLogger`[4] method that takes either a `String` or a `Class` argument. If the logger does not exist it will be automatically created.

---

[4] This method actually delegates its work to the appropriate logger repository. In other words, it is a repository that takes care of the creation and retrieval of logger instances. Log4j comes with a particular type of repository, called *hierarchy,* that arranges loggers according to the named-hierarchy rule. The only type of repository encountered in practice is the hierarchy. As such, unless specified otherwise, I will use the terms "hierarchy" and "repository" interchangeably in the remainder of this manual. The logger repository can be set by a main application such as a J2EE application server or a servlet container. The logger repository is a very advanced concept. Normally, most users neither care about nor control the logger repository they use. Chapter 8 discusses reasons for using multiple repositories. In many cases only the default hierarchy is used. At this stage you should just ignore the possibility of using multiple repositories and just assume that you are using the default repository, a.k.a. the default hierarchy.

Calling the `Logger.getLogger` method with the same name will always return a reference to the exact same logger object. This is one of the basic properties of the log4j framework. For example, in the following two statements

```
Logger x = Logger.getLogger("wombat");
Logger y = Logger.getLogger("wombat");
```

x and y refer to exactly the same logger object. It is thus possible to configure a logger and then to retrieve the same instance somewhere else in the code without passing around references. In contrast to biological parenthood, where ancestors always precede their descendants, log4j loggers can be created and configured in any order. In particular, an ancestor logger will find and link to its descendants even if it is instantiated after them.

Configuration of the log4j environment is typically done at application initialization. The preferred way is by reading a configuration file. This approach will be discussed in Chapter 3.

Log4j makes it easy to name loggers by software component. This can be accomplished by statically instantiating a logger in each class, with the logger name equal to the fully qualified name of the class. This has proven to be a useful and straightforward method of defining loggers. As the log output can be easily configured to bear the name of the generating logger, this naming strategy makes it easy to identify the origin of a log message. However, this is only one possible, albeit common, strategy for naming loggers. Log4j does not impose any restriction on the name of loggers. The user is free to name loggers as she wishes. Nevertheless, naming loggers after the class where they are located seems to be the best strategy known so far.

Levels

Logging requests are made by invoking one of the *printing methods* of a logger instance. These printing methods, namely `debug()`, `info()`, `warn()`, `error()`, `fatal()` and `log()`, are member methods of the `Logger` class. Each of these methods except the more generic `log()` method corresponds to a built-in *level*. Levels[5] are closely related to the importance of the log request as judged by the

---

[5] In previous versions of log4j, we used the term *priority* instead of *level*. Consider the two terms as synonyms. I consider the term priority to be more descriptive. However, at the time of the modification, it seemed more important to be aligned with "official" Java terminology. With hindsight, I can say that changing terminology is costly and *this* particular change was not worth the effort.

developer. The notion of levels is common to all logging libraries. For example, the venerable Unix Syslog system also refers to levels whereas Microsoft NT Event Logging refers to event types.

 To print the stack trace of an exception, you must use the printing methods taking two parameters, an `Object` (the message) and a `Throwable` (the exception). We will return to this point later in the chapter.

One of the lessons learned from Syslog was that it is not always easy to decide when to use which level. In fact, as a Syslog user, I could never fully grasp the difference between the LOG_EMERG, LOG_ALERT and LOG_CRIT levels or the difference between LOG_WARNING and LOG_NOTICE. My suspicion is that the 3 bit encoding of levels in priorities left room for exactly eight levels and the authors of Syslog made use of all the available space. This is a common pattern in network-enabled protocols which have as many options as are allowed by the space allocated in their encoding. Some of these options are not meaningful and only serve as placeholders for confusion. There is not much glory in criticizing Syslog, especially twenty-five years after its inception. During that quarter of a century the world witnessed the most feverish advances in computer technology. And yet, Syslog still runs on millions on Unix systems with great success. My wish is to see log4j share the same fate in twenty-five years.

As mentioned previously, it is not always easy to decide when to use which level. In fact, a decision needs to be made for each log statement – or on countless occasions. To ease the pain of decision, log4j deliberately offers a limited set of "self-evident" levels which I now present.

The FATAL level is rarely used and usually implies the imminent crash of the application or the relevant sub-component. The ERROR level is encountered more frequently, usually following a Java exception. Error conditions do not necessarily cause the application to crash and the application may continue to service subsequent requests. The WARN level is indicative of minor problems caused by factors external to the application such as missing or inconsistent input parameters supplied by the user.

These first three levels are associated with problems. In contrast, the INFO level is associated with significant events in the *normal* life cycle of the application. The DEBUG level is associated with minor and frequently occurring but otherwise normal events. Deciding whether an event is significant or minor depends on many factors such as the time, the application development stage, the component doing the logging and the personal tastes of the developer. In general however, the fre-

quency and volume of the events serve a useful yardstick for differentiating between the INFO and DEBUG levels.

Admittedly, even with only five levels the choice is not easy. After some discussion, most development teams set their own rules for using levels. Some teams
even decide to extend the predefined set of five levels. It is important to realize that
levels are essentially just a way to filter log requests; that is their main function.

Log4j offers many ways for filtering logging requests. After a rather abstract discussion we are ready to describe the most important filter, the logger-level filter.
This filter depends on the notion of the effective level of a logger, a term defined
below.

Loggers may be assigned levels. I say, "may" because one of the big advantages of
the log4j framework is that most loggers do not need to be assigned a level. This
greatly reduces the time spent managing logging. The set of possible levels, that is
ALL[6], DEBUG, INFO, WARN, ERROR, FATAL and OFF, are defined in the
org.apache.log4j.Level class. You are also free to define your own custom
levels by sub-classing the Level class.

The effective level of a logger is given by its assigned level, if it is assigned one.
Otherwise, if the logger has not been assigned a level, it inherits the level of its
closest ancestor with an assigned level. More formally,

Effective level of a logger

> The effective or inherited level of logger L is equal to the first non-
> null level in the logger hierarchy, starting at L and proceeding up-
> wards in the hierarchy towards the root logger.

To ensure that all loggers can eventually inherit a level, the root logger always has
an assigned level. Its level can be changed to any non-null value of type Level.

Below are four tables with various assigned and effective levels for a simple logger
hierarchy consisting of the root logger and three loggers named x, x.y and x.y.z.

---

[6] The ALL and OFF levels are intended for management purposes only. They do not have
corresponding printing methods in the Logger class. For this reason, they were omitted in
the previous discussion.

Example 2-1: Level inheritance with only root having an assigned level

Logger name	Assigned level	Effective level
root	DEBUG	DEBUG
x	none	DEBUG
x.y	none	DEBUG
x.y.z	none	DEBUG

In Example 2–1above, only the root logger is assigned a level. This level, DEBUG, is inherited by the other loggers x, x.y and x.y.z. More generally, if none of the loggers are assigned a level, then all loggers inherit the level of the root logger which is set to DEBUG by default.

Example 2-2: Level Inheritance with all loggers having an assigned level

Logger name	Assigned level	Effective level
root	DEBUG	DEBUG
x	ERROR	ERROR
x.y	INFO	INFO
x.y.z	DEBUG	DEBUG

In Example 2-2, all loggers have an assigned level. There is no need for level inheritance.

Example 2-3: Level Inheritance

Logger name	Assigned level	Effective level
root	INFO	INFO
x	DEBUG	DEBUG
x.y	none	DEBUG
x.y.z	WARN	WARN

In Example 2-3, the loggers root, x and x.y.z are assigned the levels INFO, DEBUG and WARN respectively. The logger x.y inherits its level value, DEBUG, from its parent x.

Example 2-4: Level Inheritance

Logger name	Assigned level	Effective level
root	DEBUG	DEBUG
x	ERROR	ERROR
x.y	none	ERROR
x.y.z	none	ERROR

In Example 2-4, the loggers root and x and are assigned the levels DEBUG and ERROR respectively. The loggers x.y and x.y.z inherit their level, ERROR, from their nearest parent with an assigned level, x in this case.

Logger-Level filter

By definition, the printing method determines the level of a logging request. For example, if x is a logger instance, then the statement x.info("Hello world.") is a log request of level INFO.

A log request is said to pass the logger-level filter if its level is higher than or equal to the effective level of its logger. Otherwise, the request is disabled and dropped. Keep in mind that a logger without an assigned level will inherit one from the hierarchy. The logger-level filter can be more formally stated as follows.

Logger-Level Filter

> A log request of level l_R on a logger with effective level l_E, passes the logger-level filter if and only if $l_R \geq l_E$. The request is disabled (and dropped) otherwise.

This filter is at the heart of log4j. It sets it aside from older logging libraries though most recent logging libraries now incorporate similar mechanisms. The logger-level filter depends on the ordering of levels. For the standard log4j levels, we have the following ordering: ALL < DEBUG < INFO < WARN < ERROR < FATAL < OFF. Here is the logger-level filter in action.

Example 2-5: Example of Logger Level Filter (examples/chapter2/LLF.java)

```
package chapter2;

import org.apache.log4j.Logger;
import org.apache.log4j.Level;
import org.apache.log4j.BasicConfigurator;
```

```
public class LLF {

  static public void main(String[] args) {

    BasicConfigurator.configure();

    // get a logger instance named "com.foo"
    Logger logger = Logger.getLogger("com.foo");

    // Now set its level. Usually you do not need to set the level of
    // a logger programmatically but rather in a configuration script.
    // We do it here nonetheless for the purposes of this exercise.
    logger.setLevel(Level.INFO);

    Logger barLogger = Logger.getLogger("com.foo.Bar");

    // Given that WARN is the level of this logging request whereas
    // INFO is logger's effective level, this request is enabled
    // because WARN >= INFO.
    logger.warn("Low fuel level.");

    // This request is disabled, because DEBUG < INFO.
    logger.debug("Starting search for nearest gas station.");

    // The logger instance barLogger, named "com.foo.Bar", will
    // inherit its level from the logger named "com.foo" Thus, the
    // following request is enabled because INFO >= INFO.
    barLogger.info("Located nearest gas station.");

    // This request is disabled, because DEBUG < INFO.
    barLogger.debug("Exiting gas station search");
  }
}
```

Compiling *examples/chapter2/LLF.java* and executing it should produce the following (or very similar) output on the console.

```
0 [main] WARN com.foo   - Low fuel level.
10 [main] INFO com.foo.Bar   - Located nearest gas station.
```

Since it is one of the core features of log4j, I highly recommended that you take the time to fully grasp the functioning of the logger-level filter. Experimenting on your own is likely to be helpful as well.

Hierarchy-wide Threshold Filter

Log4j allows you to set a hierarchy-wide threshold such that a request below the threshold is dropped regardless of the logger or its effective level. The hierarchy-wide threshold can be viewed as a central switch that can turn logging on or off for the entire hierarchy. For example, if you choose to set the hierarchy-wide threshold to the `INFO` level, then you have effectively disabled logging below the level such that all debug level requests will be dropped regardless of the logger and its configuration.

Although it was presented second, the hierarchy-wide threshold filter is applied prior to the logger-level filter. This has important performance implications that are further discussed later in this chapter. By default, the hierarchy-wide level is set to the `ALL` level, which is the lowest possible level. Thus, the hierarchy-wide threshold does not filter out any requests – letting the logger-level filter and subsequent filters to take charge of deciding the fate of logging requests.

Example 2-6: Hierarchy-wide threshold in action (examples/chapter2/HWT.java)

```
package chapter2;
import org.apache.log4j.Logger;
import org.apache.log4j.Level;
import org.apache.log4j.spi.LoggerRepository;
import org.apache.log4j.BasicConfigurator;

public class HWT {

  static public void main(String[] args) {

    BasicConfigurator.configure();

    Logger x = Logger.getLogger("foo.bar");
    x.setLevel(Level.INFO);

    // get the containing repository
    LoggerRepository repository = x.getLoggerRepository();

    // Set the hierarchy-wide threshold to WARN effectively disabling
    // all INFO and DEBUG requests.
    repository.setThreshold(Level.WARN);

    // This request will be dropped because the hierarchy-wide
    // threshold is set to WARN even if the logger x is enabled for
    // the INFO level.
    x.info("Dropped message.");

    // Now, let us disable all levels. This will turn off logging
    // entirely, i.e. nothing will ever log.
    repository.setThreshold(Level.OFF);

    // This FATAL level request will be dropped because all levels
    // are turned off.
    x.fatal("This is a serious message but it will also be dropped.");
```

```
    // Now, let us set the hierarchy-wide threshold to ALL, the lowest
    // possible level. All requests will now pass unhindered through
    // the hierarchy-wide filter.
    repository.setThreshold(Level.ALL);

    // This request will be logged because the hierarchy-wide
    // threshold is set to ALL and the logger x is enabled for the
    // INFO level.
    x.info("Hello world.");

    // The logger-level filter will cause the following request to be
    // dropped. Indeed, the logger level (INFO) is higher than the
    // request level (DEBUG).
    x.debug("Remember: DEBUG < INFO.");
  }
}
```

Running the HWT application will yield:

```
  0 [main] INFO foo.bar  - Hello world.
```

Normally, you do not need to set the hierarchy-wide threshold programmatically. Repositories and loggers are configured using configuration scripts. Configuration scripts are discussed in the next chapter.

Printing exceptions

In the `Logger` class you may have noticed that there are two sets of printing methods, those taking a single `Object` parameter and those taking two parameters, an `Object` plus a `Throwable`. Passing a `Throwable` instance to the first set of methods will print the name of the `Throwable` but no stack trace. To obtain a stack trace, you must use the set of methods taking two parameters, as illustrated in the next example.

Example 2-7: Printing stack traces for exceptions (examples/chapter2/PrintingEx.java)

```java
package chapter2;
import org.apache.log4j.Logger;
import org.apache.log4j.BasicConfigurator;

public class PrintingEx {

  static Logger logger = Logger.getLogger("PrintingEx");

  static public void main(String[] args) {

    BasicConfigurator.configure();
```

```
  try {
    printArray(new int[] {0,2});
  } catch(Exception e) {
    // The following statement will not print the
    // exceptions's stack trace
    logger.error(e);
  }

  try {
    printArray(new int[] {111, 222});
  } catch(Exception e) {
    // The following statement will correctly print the
    // exceptions's  stack trace. Note the two parameters.
    logger.error("Could not print integer array", e);
  }
}

static void printArray(int[] intArray) {
  int len = intArray.length;
  // The following line intentionally runs outside bounds. We
  // are using smaller or equal instead of a strict inequality.
  for(int i = 0; i <= len; i++) {
    logger.debug("Index " +i+" contains value "+intArray[i]);
  }
}
}
```

Running the `PrintingEx` application will yield the following output.

```
0 [main] DEBUG PrintingEx - Index 0 contains value 0
0 [main] DEBUG PrintingEx - Index 1 contains value 2
0 [main] ERROR PrintingEx - java.lang.ArrayIndexOutOfBoundsException
0 [main] DEBUG PrintingEx - Index 0 contains value 111
0 [main] DEBUG PrintingEx - Index 1 contains value 222
10 [main] ERROR PrintingEx - Could not print integer array
java.lang.ArrayIndexOutOfBoundsException
        at chapter2.PrintingEx.printArray(PrintingEx.java:32)
        at chapter2.PrintingEx.main(PrintingEx.java:20)
```

Novice users tend to forget to use the printing methods taking two parameters. They instead opt for the printing methods taking a single object parameter. Fortunately, most users quickly adapt to this log4j idiosyncrasy. Log4j developers could have easily modified the API to check for the type of the message parameter in order to print the stack trace if it was of the type `Throwable`. However, our belief is that requiring a message parameter in addition to the exception, encourages good practice, whereby each exception stack trace is preceded by an explanatory message.

Appenders

The ability to selectively filter out logging requests is only one part of the picture. In addition, log4j allows logging requests to print to multiple destinations. In log4j speak an output destination is called an *appender*. Currently, appenders exist for the console, files, Swing components, remote socket servers, JMS, NT Event Loggers, and remote UNIX Syslog daemons. It is also possible to log asynchronously. If you need to log to a particular output device, chances are good that someone has already written a log4j appender for that device even if it is not difficult to write your own appender suited for your particular needs.

Log4j allows attaching multiple appenders to any logger. Appenders can be added to and removed from a logger at any time. The central architectural concept in log4j is the hierarchical arrangement of loggers. As explained previously, loggers inherit their effective level from the hierarchy. A logger can make use of one and only one level. Appenders are different because multiple appenders can be attached to a logger. It makes sense to inherit appenders attached to higher loggers in a child logger. What should be the logic of appender inheritance according to your judgment?

Appender Additivity

Invoking the `addAppender` method (see the `Logger` class) adds an appender to a given logger. Each enabled logging request for a given logger will be forwarded to all the appenders in that logger, as well as the appenders higher in the hierarchy. In other words, appenders are inherited *additively* from the logger hierarchy. For example, if a console appender is added to the root logger, then all enabled logging requests will at least print on the console. If in addition a file appender is added to a logger, say *L*, then enabled logging requests for *L* and *L*'s descendants will print on a file *and* on the console. It is possible to override this default behavior so that appender accumulation is no longer additive by setting the additivity flag to false.

The rule governing appender additivity is summarized below.

Appender Additivity Rule

> The output of a log statement of some logger *L* is forwarded to all the appenders in *L and* its ancestors. This is the meaning of the term "appender additivity."
>
> However, if an ancestor of logger *L*, say *P*, has its additivity flag set to false, then *L*'s output will be directed to all the appenders in *L* and its ancestors up to and including *P*, but not the appenders in any of the ancestors of *P*.
>
> Loggers have their additivity flag set to true by default.

Log4j configuration is declarative. This means that the end-user normally does not manipulate appenders programmatically but through configuration files. For educational purposes, the next example programmatically instantiates two separate file appenders and adds them to the root logger.

Example 2-8: Attaching appenders to loggers (examples/chapter2/AppendEx1.java)

```
package chapter2;

import org.apache.log4j.Logger;
import org.apache.log4j.FileAppender;
import org.apache.log4j.SimpleLayout;

public class AppenderEx1 {

  static public void main(String[] args) throws Exception {

      FileAppender a0 = new FileAppender(new SimpleLayout(), "a0.log");
      FileAppender a1 = new FileAppender(new SimpleLayout(), "a1.log");

      Logger root = Logger.getRootLogger();
      root.addAppender(a0);

      Logger x = Logger.getLogger("x");
      x.addAppender(a1);

      Logger xyz = Logger.getLogger("x.y.z");

      // Note that we have not added any appenders to the xyz logger.
      xyz.debug("Some message.");
      xyz.info("Another message.");
  }
}
```

Executing java *chapter2.AppenderEx1* will create two files *a0.log* and *a1.log* containing the following text.

```
DEBUG - Some message.
INFO - Another message.
```

Notice that the two log requests are made using the "xyz" logger but the output is nevertheless directed to the appenders attached to the "x" and root loggers. This example demonstrates the additive manner in which appenders are inherited. You are probably wondering about the two lines instantiating the two `FileAppender` objects. The first parameter to the `FileAppender` is a *layout*. Layouts will be introduced shortly. The second parameter is the name of the file to write to.

The next example demonstrates the effects of setting the additivity flag of a logger to false.

Example 2-9: Additivity flag (examples/chapter2/AppendEx2.java)

```java
package chapter2;

import org.apache.log4j.Logger;
import org.apache.log4j.FileAppender;
import org.apache.log4j.SimpleLayout;

public class AppenderEx2 {

  static public void main(String[] args) throws Exception {

    FileAppender a0 = new FileAppender(new SimpleLayout(), "a0.log");
    FileAppender a1 = new FileAppender(new SimpleLayout(), "a1.log");
    FileAppender secureAppender = new FileAppender(new SimpleLayout(),
                                        "secret.log");

    Logger root = Logger.getRootLogger();
    root.addAppender(a0);

    Logger x = Logger.getLogger("x");
    x.addAppender(a1);

    Logger xyz = Logger.getLogger("x.y.z");

    Logger secureLogger = Logger.getLogger("secure");
    secureLogger.addAppender(secureAppender);
    secureLogger.setAdditivity(false);

    // The accessLogger is a child of the secureLogger.
    Logger accessLogger = Logger.getLogger("secure.access");

    // Output goes to a0.log and a1.log.
    xyz.debug("Regular message.");
```

```
    // Output goes only to secret.log.
    accessLogger.warn("Detected snooping attempt by Eve.");
  }
}
```

After executing sample application *chapter2.AppenderEx2*, you should find the following text

```
    WARN - Detected snooping attempt by Eve.
```

in the *secret.log* file, but this text will not be present in *a0.log* or *a1.log* because the additivity flag of `secureLogger` (the parent of `accessLogger`) has been set to false. It goes without saying that appender additivity applies to appenders of all types even if we just used file appenders in the above examples.

Layouts

More often than not, users wish to customize not only the output destination but also the output format. This is accomplished by associating a *layout* with an appender. The layout is responsible for formatting the logging request according to the user's wishes, whereas an appender takes care of sending formatted output to its destination. Most layouts are not designed to be shared by multiple appenders. It follows that each appender must have its own "private" layout.

A common layout called the `PatternLayout`, part of the standard log4j distribution, lets the user specify the output format according to conversion patterns similar to the C language's `printf` function. For example, a `PatternLayout` with the conversion pattern "%r [%t] %-5p %c - %m%n" will output something akin to:

```
    176 [main] INFO  org.wombat.Bar - Located nearest gas station.
```

The first field is the number of milliseconds elapsed since the start of the program. The second field is the thread that executed the log request. The third field is the level of the log statement. The fourth field is the name of the logger associated with the log request. The text after the '-' is the message of the statement. Specific configuration parameters for layouts, including the `PatternLayout`, will be discussed in later chapters.

Object Rendering

Object rendering is a powerful and unique log4j feature. Log4j will render the content of the log messages according to user specified criteria. For example, if you frequently need to log oranges, an object type used in your current project, then you can register an `OrangeRenderer` that will be invoked whenever an orange object is passed as the message parameter in a logging statement. The previously registered `OrangeRenderer` will be invoked to render a string representation of orange objects. Here is an (incomplete) example of how object rendering might work.

```
Orange orange = new Orange("89", "jaffa");
logger.debug("Here is how a rendered orange looks:");
logger.debug(orange);
```

Here is a possible outcome assuming the appropriate renderer and object types were properly registered.

```
4309 DEBUG [main] example.orange - Here is how a rendered orange looks:
4312 DEBUG [main] example.orange - jaffa brand, weighing 89 grams.
```

Object rendering follows the class hierarchy. For example, assuming oranges are fruits, if you register a `FruitRenderer`, all fruits including oranges will be rendered by the `FruitRenderer`, unless of course you registered an orange specific `OrangeRenderer`.

Object renderers are required to implement the `org.apache.log4j.or.-ObjectRenderer` interface. Log4j comes with a few useful renderers. For example, you can use the `AttributesRenderer`[7] to render `org.xml.sax.-Attributes` objects.

A Peek under the Hood

After we have introduced the essential log4j components, we are now ready to describe the steps that the log4j framework takes when the user invokes a logger's printing method. Let us now analyze the steps log4j takes when the user invokes the `info()` method of a logger named "com.wombat".

1. Hierarchy-wide threshold check

Every single logger has a reference to the repository that created it. A logger will drop the request and immediately exit the printing method if the repository is not enabled for the request level, `INFO` in this particular case. The hierarchy-wide threshold was discussed earlier in this chapter. The cost of this test is just a method invocation and an integer comparison – in other words extremely low, usually less than a dozen nanoseconds (10^{-9} sec).

---

[7] The `AttributesRenderer` class is located in the org.apache.log4j.or.sax package.

2. Apply the Logger-Level filter

Next, log4j compares the effective level of the "com.wombat" logger with the level of the request (INFO) by applying the logger-level filter. If the logging request is disabled, then log4j will drop the request without any further processing and exit the printing method, `Logger.info()` in this case.

3. Creating a LoggingEvent object

If the request is enabled, then log4j will create a `org.apache.log4j.spi.-LoggingEvent` object containing all the relevant parameters of the request such as the logger of the request, the level of the request, the message as an object, the current thread and the current time. Other fields are initialized lazily, that is only when they are actually needed. The `LoggingEvent` class is described in more detail in the next section.

4. Invoking appenders

After the creation of a `LoggingEvent` object, log4j will proceed to invoke the `doAppend()` methods of all the applicable appenders, that is, the appenders inherited from the logger hierarchy.

All appenders shipped with the log4j distribution extend the `AppenderSkeleton` abstract class that implements the `doAppend` method in a synchronized block ensuring thread-safety. The `doAppend` method of `AppenderSkeleton` also invokes *custom filters* attached to the appender, if any such filters exist. Custom filters, which can be dynamically attached to any appender, will be presented Chapter 6.

5. Formatting the LoggingEvent

It is responsibility of the invoked appender to format the logging event. However, most (but not all) appenders delegate the task of formatting the logging event to their layout. Their layout formats the `LoggingEvent` instance and returns the result as a `String`. The formatting of event *message* (but not the whole logging event) is usually delegated to object renderers of the logger repository. Note that some appenders, such as the `SocketAppender`, do not transform the logging event into a string but serialize it instead. Consequently, they do not require nor have a layout.

6. Sending out the LoggingEvent

After the logging event is fully formatted it is sent to its destination by each appender. See also step 4.

LoggingEvent class

After a logging request passes the hierarchy-wide threshold and the logger-level filter, although not absolutely certain, the chances are high that the log request will be ultimately written to some medium. After these two verifications, log4j creates a LoggingEvent[8] object, log4j's internal representation of log requests. We talk about a *logging event* when discussing log4j internals, whereas we use the term *logging request* to refer to the invocation of log4j printing methods by the user. Consider the two terms as quasi-synonyms used interchangeably in the text.

Some of the fields composing a LoggingEvent object are assigned within the object constructor. These fields are the level of the request, the logger, the current time, the message parameter passed by the user and the associated throwable if any. The current time is a value returned by System.currentTimeMillis() method which corresponds to the number of milliseconds elapsed since midnight, January 1st, 1970 UTC. This value is locale independent. Ignoring drifts in their respective clocks, two logging events generated at the same instant on two computers in different time zones, possibly thousands of kilometers apart, will bear the same timestamp.

Other fields such as the thread name, NDC, MDC and LocationInformation are initialized lazily, that is when accessed for the first time. The NDC and MDC fields are discussed in later chapters. LocationInformation is log4j's internal representation of the caller's location which includes the caller's file name, line number and class name. The location information is extracted from the program execution stack in a relatively slow and time consuming process. Moreover, location information may not always be available because certain just-in-time compilers and other code optimizers modify the structure of the execution stack.

LoggingEvent is serializable class. This allows a logging event instance created on one computer to be logged remotely on a different computer. The remote host can manipulate a deserialized event as if it were generated locally. Reading the source code of the LoggingEvent class you may have noticed that several of its fields are marked public which is contrary to object-oriented design principles. If you look more carefully, you will see that several of these fields are marked as final public, allowing any class to access these fields directly but not to modify them. For various and involved technical reasons, the level field is marked as

---

[8] The LoggingEvent class is located in the org.apache.log4j.spi package.

`transient public`. This combination means that it is read/write accessible by everyone but not serialized. Thus, any class can modify the level of an event. However, `LoggingEvent` objects are only visible to certain appenders[9] or to their associated layouts. In theory, a rogue appender could modify the logger or level of an event. Thus far, this has never been a problem although a malicious appender or layout could take advantage of this vulnerability. It is hard to imagine an exploit based on this vulnerability. Nevertheless, one can never be completely sure. In any case, make sure to verify the origin of any appender used in a sensitive application. In future log4j releases, the level field will be marked as private, restraining its accessibility to accessor methods.

Performance

One of the often-cited arguments against logging is its computational cost. This is a legitimate concern as even moderately sized applications can generate thousands of log requests. Much effort was spent measuring and tweaking logging performance. Log4j claims to be reliable, fast and extensible – in that order of priority. Independently of these efforts, the user should still be aware of the following performance issues.

1.   Logging performance when logging is turned off entirely.

You can turn off logging entirely by setting the threshold of a repository to `Level.OFF`, the highest possible level. See *Hierarchy-wide Threshold* on page 29 on how to set the threshold of a repository. When logging is turned off entirely or for a level below the threshold, the cost of a log request consists of a method invocation plus an integer comparison. On a 233 MHz Pentium II machine this cost is typically in the 5 to 50 nanosecond range.

However, any method invocation involves the "hidden" cost of parameter construction. For example, for some logger x writing,

```
    x.debug("Entry number: " +i+" is "+entry[i]);
```

incurs the cost of constructing the message parameter, i.e. converting both integer i and entry[i] to a string, and concatenating intermediate strings, regardless of whether the message will be logged or not.

---

[9] More specifically, a `LoggingEvent` is accessible to those appenders which are attached to any of the loggers on the hierarchical path of the logger which created the `LoggingEvent`.

The cost of parameter construction can be quite high and depends on the size of the parameters involved. To avoid the cost of parameter construction you can write:

```
if(x.isDebugEnabled() {
   x.debug("Entry number: "+i+" is "+String.valueOf(entry[i]));
}
```

This will not incur the cost of parameter construction if the DEBUG level is disabled. On the other hand, if the logger is debug-enabled, it will twice incur the cost of evaluating whether the logger is enabled or not: once in isDebugEnabled() and once in debug(). This is an insignificant overhead because evaluating a logger takes less than 1% of the time it actually takes to log. If a method contains multiple log statements, it may be possible to factor out the tests. Here is an example:

```
public void foo(Object[] a) {
   boolean debug = x.isDebugEnabled();

   for(int i = 0; i < a.length; i++) {
     if(debug)
        x.debug("Original value of entry number: "+i+" is "+a[i]);

     a[i] = someTransformation(a[i]);
     if(debug)
        x.debug("After transformation the value is "+a[i]);
   }
}
```

In addition to the isDebugEnabled method, the Logger class contains the is-InfoEnabled and isEnabledFor methods. The isInfoEnabled method allows us to check whether or not a given logger is enabled for the INFO level. The isEnabledFor computes whether a given logger is enabled for the level passed as parameter. Note that there are no specific isEnabled methods for WARN, ERROR and FATAL levels. Given the relative rarity logging statements of WARN, ERROR or FATAL levels, the existence of isEnabled methods for these levels cannot be justified by performance considerations.

In log4j, logging requests are made to instances of the Logger class. Logger is a class and not an interface. This measurably reduces the cost of method invocation at the cost of some flexibility, although in some recent JVMs, the performance difference became negligible.

Certain users resort to preprocessing or compile-time techniques to compile out all log statements. Most java compilers, including *javac* and *jikes*, will remove conditional statements which are assured to always evaluate as false. In the next example, the compiler will remove the dead if statement in the foo method by compiling it as an immediately returning method.

Example 2-10:Factoring out dead log statements (examples/chapter3/FactorOut.java)

```
package chapter2;

import org.apache.log4j.Logger;

public class FactorOut {
    static final boolean D = false;
    static Logger logger = Logger.getLogger(FactorOut.class);

    void foo(int i) {
        if(D) logger.debug("Input parameter is :"+ i);
    }
}
```

Compile the `FactorOut` class with any java compiler. Disassemble the resulting class by running *javap*, the standard Java Class File Disassembler shipped with the JDK:

```
javap -c chapter2.FactorOut
```

This will yield byte code information for the `foo` method, (cut to fit):

```
Method void foo(int)
   0 return
```

In other words, the compiler was able to weed out and eliminate the dead `if` statement. Note that if the D static variable were not final, the compiler could not have optimized the `if` statement. The `foo` method would instead disassemble as:

```
Method void foo(int)
  0 getstatic #7 <Field boolean D>
  3 ifeq 31
  6 getstatic #8 <Field org.apache.log4j.Logger logger>
  9 new #9 <Class java.lang.StringBuffer>
 12 dup
 13 invokespecial #10 <Method java.lang.StringBuffer()>
 16 ldc #11 <String "Input parameter is :">
 18 invokevirtual #12 <Method java.lang.StringBuffer ap-
pend(java.lang.String)>
 21 iload_1
 22 invokevirtual #13 <Method java.lang.StringBuffer append(int)>
 25 invokevirtual #14 <Method java.lang.String toString()>
 28 invokevirtual #15 <Method void debug(java.lang.Object)>
 31 return
```

Such final static variables need not be present in each class file. One can conveniently place them in a single class and import it in other classes. As long as the conditional expression is guaranteed to be false, the compiler will eliminate dead `if` statements. Section 14.19 of the Java Language specification, entitled "Un-

reachable Statements," requires that every java compiler carry out conservative
flow analysis to make sure all statements are reachable. Compilers are required to
report an error if a statement cannot be executed because it is unreachable. Interestingly enough, `if` statements are a special case. In contrast to other unreachable
statements, unreachable `if` statements do not generate compile time errors, In fact,
the authors of the specification explicitly state that this behavior is required in order to support conditional compilation. The same section also warns that "condi-
tionally compilation" has significant impact on binary compatibility. For example,
if classes A, B, and C import a flag variable form class F, then changing the value of
the flag variable and compiling F will *not* impact the already compiled versions of
A, B, and C. Beware of this problem if your classes are compiled selectively.

The conditional compilation technique leads to perfect performance efficiency with
respect to logging. However, since the resulting application binary does not contain
any log statements, logging cannot be turned on for that binary. This is perhaps a
disproportionate price to pay in exchange for a (possibly) small performance gain.
The performance gain will be significant only if log statements are placed in tight-
loops where the same log request is invoked potentially millions or even billions of
times. Inserting logging statements in tight-loops is a lose-lose proposal. They will
slow down your application even if logging is turned off or generate massive (and
hence useless) logging output if enabled.

 Inserting logging statements in tight-loops or very frequently invoked
code is a lose-lose proposal. They will slow down your application
even if logging is turned off or generate massive (and hence useless)
output if enabled.

2. The performance of deciding whether to log or not to log when logging is turned on.

This is essentially the performance of walking the logger hierarchy. When logging
is turned on, log4j still needs to compare the level of the log request with the level
of the request logger. However, loggers may not have an assigned level; they can
inherit them from the logger hierarchy. Thus, before inheriting a level, the logger
may need to search its ancestors.

There has been a serious effort to make this hierarchy walk to be as fast as possible. For example, child loggers link only to their existing ancestors. This signifi-
cantly improves the speed of the walk, especially in "sparse" hierarchies.

The cost of walking the hierarchy is typically 3 times slower than just checking whether logging is turned off entirely.

3.   Actual logging (formatting and writing to the output device).

This is the cost of formatting the log output and sending it to its target destination. Here again, a serious effort was made to make layouts (formatters) perform as quickly as possible. The same is true for appenders. The typical cost of actually logging is about 100 to 300 microseconds. See `org.apache.log4j.per-formance.Logging` for actual figures.

Although feature-rich, one of the foremost design goals of log4j was *speed* of execution, a requirement which is second only to *reliability*. Some log4j components have been rewritten many times to improve performance. Nevertheless, contributors frequently come up with new optimizations. You should be pleased to know that when configured with the `SimpleLayout`, performance tests have shown log4j to log as quickly as `System.out.println`[10].

Now that you have an understanding of loggers, their hierarchical nature, levels, appenders, layouts and other log4j building blocks, the next chapter will show you to configure log4j declaratively with the help of configuration scripts.

---

[10] Given that on Windows NT printing on the console is rather slow, the performance tests were done on a screen with a window size of just one row. This considerably accelerates the output rate of the console.

3

CONFIGURATION SCRIPTS

*In symbols one observes an advantage in discovery
which is greatest when they express the exact nature
of a thing briefly and, as it were, picture it; then indeed the labor of thought is wonderfully diminished.*

—GOTTFRIED WILHELM LEIBNIZ

Inserting log requests into the application code requires a fair amount of planning
and effort. My observations show that approximately 4 percent of code is dedicated
to logging. Consequently, even moderately sized applications will have thousands
of logging statements embedded within their source code. Given their number, it
becomes imperative to manage these log statements without the need to modify
them manually.

The log4j environment is fully configurable programmatically. However, it is far
more flexible to configure log4j using configuration files. Currently, configuration
files can be written Java properties (key=value) format or in XML. In this chapter I
will give examples of log4j configuration files expressed in properties (key=value)
format and in XML format.

Simplest approach using BasicConfigurator

As mentioned in Chapter 1, the simplest way to configure log4j is by using `Ba-
sicConfigurator.configure()` method. Let us give a taste of how this is
done with the help of an imaginary application called *MyApp1*.

*Example 3-1: Simple example of BasicConfigurator usage (examples/chapter3/-
MyApp1.java)*

```
package chapter3;
import org.apache.log4j.Logger;
import org.apache.log4j.BasicConfigurator;
```

```
public class MyApp1 {

  final static Logger logger = Logger.getLogger(MyApp1.class);

  public static void main(String[] args) {

    //Set up a simple configuration that logs on the console.
    BasicConfigurator.configure();

    logger.info("Entering application.");
    Foo foo = new Foo();
    foo.doIt();
    logger.info("Exiting application.");
  }
}
```

MyApp1 begins by importing log4j related classes. It then defines a static logger
variable with the name "chapter3.MyApp" by invoking the `Logger.getLogger`
method. This variant of the `getLogger` method takes a `Class` parameter. The returned logger will have the fully qualified class name of the class parameter.
MyApp1 uses the `Foo` class defined in the same package, as listed below.

```
package chapter3;
import org.apache.log4j.Logger;

public class Foo {
  static final Logger logger = Logger.getLogger(Foo.class);

  public void doIt() {
    logger.debug("Did it again!");
  }
}
```

Invoking of the `BasicConfigurator.configure()` method creates a rather
simple log4j setup. This method is hardwired to add a `ConsoleAppender` to the
root logger. The output is formatted using a `PatternLayout` set to the pattern "%-
4r [%t] %-5p %c %x - %m%n". Note that by default the root logger is assigned to
the DEBUG level.

The output of the command **java chapter3.MyApp1** should be similar to:

```
0 [main] INFO chapter3.MyApp1  - Entering application.
0 [main] DEBUG chapter3.Foo  - Did it again!
0 [main] INFO chapter3.MyApp1  - Exiting application.
```

If you are unable to run this command, then make sure that your CLASSPATH
environment variable is setup properly. Refer to the section entitled "Running the
Examples" on page 16 for more details.

The figure below depicts the object diagram of *MyApp1* after just having called the `BasicConfigurator.configure()` method.

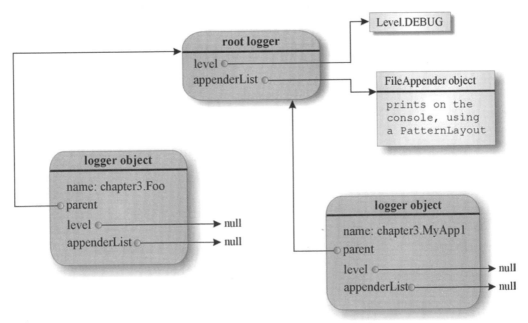

Figure 3-1: Object diagram for the log4j hierarchy in MyApp1.

As a side note, let me mention that in log4j child loggers link only to their existing ancestors. In particular, the logger named "chapter3.Foo" is linked directly with the root logger, thereby circumventing the unused "chapter3" logger. This noticeably improves the performance of hierarchy walks and also slightly reduces log4j's memory footprint.

The `MyApp1` class configures log4j by invoking `BasicConfigura-tor.configure()` method. All other classes only need to import the `org.apache.log4j.Logger` class, retrieve the loggers they wish to use, and log away. For example, the only dependence of the `Foo` class on log4j is the `org.apache.log4j.Logger` import. Except code that configures log4j (if such code exists) user code does not need to depend on log4j except for the `Logger` class. Given that the `java.util.logging` API enjoys a similar property; it is rather easy to migrate large bodies of code from `java.util.logging` to log4j, or vice versa, at the stroke of just a few simple string search-and-replace operations.

The same using PropertyConfigurator

The previous example outputs logging information always in the same fixed manner. Fortunately, it is easy to modify *MyApp1* so that the log output can be controlled at run-time. Here is a slightly modified version called *MyApp2*.

Example 3-2: The same using PropertyConfigurator (examples/chapter3/MyApp2.java)

```
package chapter3;

import org.apache.log4j.Logger;
import org.apache.log4j.PropertyConfigurator;

public class MyApp2 {

  final static Logger logger = Logger.getLogger(MyApp2.class);

  public static void main(String[] args) {

    PropertyConfigurator.configure(args[0]);

    logger.info("Entering application.");
    Foo foo = new Foo();
    foo.doIt();
    logger.info("Exiting application.");
  }
}
```

MyApp2 instructs `PropertyConfigurator` to parse a configuration file and to set up logging according to the instructions found therein. The sample configuration file listed below, also available as *examples/chapter3/sample0.properties*, configures log4j (after parsing by `PropertyConfigurator`) in the same way as `BasicConfigurator.configure`.

Example   3-3:   BasicConfigurator.configure()   equivalent   (examples/chapter3/-sample0.properties)

```
# Set root logger level to DEBUG and add an appender called A1.
log4j.rootLogger=DEBUG, A1

# A1 is set to be a ConsoleAppender.
log4j.appender.A1=org.apache.log4j.ConsoleAppender

# A1 uses PatternLayout.
log4j.appender.A1.layout=org.apache.log4j.PatternLayout
log4j.appender.A1.layout.ConversionPattern=%-4r [%t] %-5p %c %x - %m%n
```

Assuming the current directory is *LOG4J_MANUAL/examples*, try executing the following command:

```
java chapter3.MyApp2 chapter3/sample0.properties
```

The output of this command is very similar to the output of the previous example, except that *MyApp2* retrieves a logger called "chapter3.MyApp2" instead of "chapter3.MyApp1". The output will reflect this difference.

It is often very useful to define the **log4j.debug** system property in order to instruct log4j to output internal debugging messages on the console. As in:

```
java -Dlog4j.debug chapter3.MyApp2 chapter3/sample0.properties
```

This should cause log4j to print internal debugging messages in addition to the actual logs. Another way to instruct log4j to print internal debugging messages is to define the log4j.debug property within the configuration file. As in:

```
log4j.debug=true
log4j.rootLogger=DEBUG, A1
log4j.appender.A1=org.apache.log4j.ConsoleAppender

... etc.
```

Internal log4j messages only appear on the console. As of this writing, the internal debug messages cannot be redirected to output devices other than the console. The limitation stems from the fact that log4j cannot use itself to perform its own logging. This can be considered as an intriguing architectural flaw which we intend to address in future versions of log4j. Fortunately enough, it seems that this limitation has not had any practical impact.

Syntax of Configuration Files in Properties format

A property configuration file consists of statements in the format "key=value". Configuration files are fed to a `PropertyConfigurator` instance which parses them and configures log4j accordingly. A sample configuration file reproducing the `BasicConfigurator.configure` behavior was given previously. More interesting and useful examples will be given shortly. However, before delving into examples, a more formal definition of the property file format is in order. Armed with the knowledge about the expected syntax, you will be able to define elaborate configuration files of your own. In the syntax definitions below *constant width italic* elements represent replaceable elements supplied by the user. Elements between brackets represent optional elements.

Note that the `PropertyConfigurator` does not handle some advanced configuration features supported in XML format, such as filter chains, custom error handling, or nested appenders (e.g. `AsyncAppender`).

Setting the hierarchy-wide threshold

The repository-wide threshold filters logging requests by level, regardless of the logger. The syntax is:

```
log4j.threshold=level
```

The level value can consist of the case-insensitive string values "OFF", "FATAL", "ERROR", "WARN", "INFO", "DEBUG", "ALL" or a custom level value. A custom level[11] value can be specified in the form "level#classname". The quote characters are not required and must be omitted in actual configuration files, as illustrated in the following examples.

The following directive disables all logging for the entire hierarchy.

```
log4j.threshold=OFF
```

The following directive disables logging for all the levels below the WARN level such that logging request of levels INFO and DEBUG are dropped for all loggers regardless of their effective level.

```
log4j.threshold=WARN
```

The following directive sets the hierarchy-wide threshold to ALL, such that all requests are necessarily above the threshold.

```
log4j.threshold=ALL
```

By default the repository-wide threshold is set to the lowest possible value, namely the level ALL. In other words, the hierarchy-wide threshold is inactive by default, letting all logging requests to pass through to the next filter.

Appender configuration

Appenders are named entities. Appender names can contain any character except the equals '=' character. Although discouraged, appender names can contain dots

---

[11] We shall discuss custom levels in detail in Chapter 8 "Extending log4j."

which do not assume any particular meaning in this context. The first step in configuring an appender is to specify its name and class:

```
# Specify the appender name as well as its class.
log4j.appender.appenderName=fully.qualified.name.of.appender.class
```

This has the effect of instantiating an appender of the specified class and set the name of the appender instance. The next step is to set the options of the appender. The syntax is:

```
log4j.appender.appenderName.option1=value1
log4j.appender.appenderName.option2=value2
...
log4j.appender.appenderName.optionN=valueN
```

The *options*, a.k.a. *properties*, of an appender are inferred dynamically using the well known JavaBeans paradigm. Any setter method taking a single primitive java type, an `Integer`, a `Long`, a `String` or a `Boolean` parameter corresponds to an option (property). For example, given that the `FileAppender` class contains `setAppend(boolean)`, `setBufferSize(int)` and `setFile(String)` as member methods, then it follows that **Append**, **BufferSize** and **File** are all valid option names. Log4j can also deal with setter methods taking a parameter of type `org.apache.log4j.Level`. For example, since the `AppenderSkeleton` class[12] has `setThreshold(Level)` as a member method, **Threshold** is a valid option for all log4j appenders extending `AppenderSkeleton`. Thus, even without a formal list for the options of a given appender, it is easy to discover the options supported by an appender by examining its setter methods as well as those in its super classes.

For each named appender you can also configure its layout. The syntax for configuring a layout for a given named appender is shown next.

```
log4j.appender.appenderName.layout=fully.qualified.name.of.layout.class
```

This has the effect of instantiating a layout of the specified class and attaching it to the named appender instantiated earlier. In contrast to appenders which are named entities, layouts do not have names as they do not need to be addressed individually. A layout is associated with one and only one appender.

---

[12] The `AppenderSkeleton` class is the base class for all appenders shipped in the official log4j distribution.

Configuring loggers

After appenders and their associated layouts were specified, you can attach them to loggers. In the most typical case, appenders are attached to the root logger. The syntax for configuring the root logger is:

```
log4j.rootLogger=[level] [, appenderName1, appenderName2, ...]
```

The above syntax means that an optional level can be followed by optional appender names separated by commas. The level value can consist of the case-insensitive string values "OFF", "FATAL", "ERROR", "WARN", "INFO", "DEBUG", "ALL" or a custom level value. A custom level value can be specified in the form "level#classname". The quote characters surrounding these string values are not required and must be omitted in actual configuration files.

If a level value is specified, then the root level is set to the corresponding level. If no level value is specified, then the level of the root logger remains untouched. Multiple appenders can be attached to any logger, including the root logger. Each named appender mentioned in the root logger directive will be added to the root logger. However, before adding these appenders, all the appenders previously attached to root logger are closed and then detached.

For non-root categories the syntax is almost the same:

```
log4j.logger.loggerName=[level|INHERITED|NULL] [, appenderName1,
appenderName2, ...]
```

where *loggerName* corresponds to the name of the logger you wish to configure. There are no restrictions on logger names.

In addition to the level values allowed for the root logger, non-root loggers admit the case-insensitive string value "INHERITED", or its synonym "NULL". These values have the effect of setting the logger's level to null. Note that in actual configuration files the quote characters around "INHERITED" and "NULL" are unnecessary and must be omitted.

If no level value is supplied, then the level of the named logger remains untouched. By default loggers inherit their level from the hierarchy. However, if you set the level of a logger and later decide that the logger should inherit its level, then you should specify "NULL" or "INHERITED" as the level value.

Similar to the root logger syntax, each named appender will be attached to the named logger. However, before attaching these new appenders any previously attached appenders to the named logger are first closed and then detached from the named logger.

The syntax for setting the additivity flag of a logger is:

```
log4j.additivity.loggerName=[true|false]
```

Contrary to what one might expect, the "additivity" keyword appears before the logger name and not after. There is a rationale for this idiosyncrasy. By design all logger names are considered valid, in particular a name that ends with ".additivity" – a very unlikely case but one that still must be taken into consideration. The additivity flag applies only to non-root loggers because the root logger, placed at the top of the hierarchy by construction, has no parent loggers.

ObjectRenderers

Object renderers, introduced on page 36, allow you to customize the way message objects of a given type are converted to string before being logged. This is done by specifying an `ObjectRenderer` for the object type would like to customize. The syntax for specifying object renderers is as follows.

```
log4j.renderer.fqnOfRenrederedClass=fqnOfRenrederingClass
```

where FQN stands for fully qualified name. The following directive instructs log4j to apply the `chapter3.FruitRenderer` for log messages of type `chapter3.-Fruit`.

```
log4j.renderer.chapter3.Fruit=chapter3.FruitRenderer
```

A sample configuration file *objectRendering.properties* can be found under the *examples/chapter3/* directory. See also the source files *ObjectRenderingSample.java, Fruit.java* and *Orange.java* in the same directory for a simple example of object rendering.

Variable substitution

All option *values* admit variable substitution. The syntax of variable substitution is similar to that of Unix shells. The string between an opening "**${**" and closing "**}**" is interpreted as a key. The value of the substituted variable can be defined as a system property or in the configuration file itself. The value of the key is first searched in the system properties, and if not found there, it is then searched in the configuration file being parsed. The corresponding value replaces `${aKey}` sequence. For example, if `java.home` system property is set to `/home/xyz`, then every occurrence of the sequence `${java.home}` will be interpreted as `/home/xyz`. Recursive substitution is also supported as the next script illustrates.

Example 3-4: Variable substitution (examples/chapter3/substitution.properties)

```
dir=${user.home}
file=test.log
target=${dir}/${file}
log4j.debug=true
log4j.rootLogger=debug, TEST
log4j.appender.TEST=org.apache.log4j.FileAppender
log4j.appender.TEST.File=${target}
log4j.appender.TEST.layout=org.apache.log4j.PatternLayout
log4j.appender.TEST.layout.ConversionPattern=%p %t %c - %m%n
```

Running *MyApp2* with this script will output log messages into a file named *test.log* in your home directory. The file name is build from the value of the `target` variable composed by the concatenation of the `dir` and `file` variables. The `dir` variable is itself built from the value of the `user.home` system property. For equivalent results, we could have also written:

```
log4j.debug=true
log4j.rootLogger=debug, TEST
log4j.appender.TEST=org.apache.log4j.FileAppender
log4j.appender.TEST.File=${user.home}/test.log
log4j.appender.TEST.layout=org.apache.log4j.PatternLayout
log4j.appender.TEST.layout.ConversionPattern=%p %t %c - %m%n
```

Setting the hierarchy-wide threshold

The fastest but also the least flexible way of filtering logging statements is by setting a hierarchy-wide threshold. This approach was explained in detail in the current as well as previous chapters. It is quite easy to set the repository-wide threshold in a configuration file. This is illustrated in the sample configuration file listed below.

Example 3-5: Setting the hierarchy-wide threshold to WARN *(examples/chapter3/-sample1.properties)*

```
log4j.rootLogger=DEBUG, CON
log4j.appender.CON=org.apache.log4j.ConsoleAppender
log4j.appender.CON.layout=org.apache.log4j.PatternLayout

log4j.appender.CON.layout.ConversionPattern=[%t] %-5p %c - %m%n

#Limit printing to level WARN or above for all loggers
log4j.threshold=WARN
```

As *MyApp2* does not contain any warn, error or fatal log statements, running the *MyApp2* application with the *sample1.properties* configuration file will not produce any logging output.

Setting the level of a logger

The central feature of any logging library is support for filtering logging messages based on diverse criteria. One of the core features of log4j is its ability to filter log statements by a logger's effective level as discussed in section "Logger-Level filter" on page 28.

Suppose we are no longer interested in seeing any INFO or DEBUG level logs from any component belonging to the "chapter3" package. The following configuration file illustrates a succinct way for achieving this.

Example 3-6: Setting the level of chapter3 logger to WARN (examples/chapter3-/sample2.properties)

```
log4j.rootLogger=DEBUG, CON
log4j.appender.CON=org.apache.log4j.ConsoleAppender
log4j.appender.CON.layout=org.apache.log4j.PatternLayout

log4j.appender.CON.layout.ConversionPattern=[%t] %-5p %c - %m%n

# Print only messages of priority WARN or above in package "chapter3".
log4j.logger.chapter3=WARN
```

This configuration file sets the level of the logger named "chapter3" to WARN. In general, every logger which is mentioned in a configuration is retrieved by calling the Logger.getLogger() method with the logger name passed as argument. Recall that calling the Logger.getLogger() method multiple times with the same name argument will return a reference to exactly the same logger instance. Interestingly enough, the Java source code in *MyApp2* does not refer directly to a logger named "chapter3". However, as a direct result of the named hierarchy rule, this logger is the parent of the "chapter3.MyApp2"and "chapter3.Foo" loggers. As such, these loggers automatically inherit the WARN level.

The following table summarizes the assigned and effective levels of the relevant loggers after PropertyConfigurator configures log4j using the *sample2.properties* file.

Logger name	Assigned level	Effective level
root	DEBUG	DEBUG
chapter3	WARN	WARN
chapter3.MyApp2	null	WARN
chapter3.Foo	null	WARN

Consequently, log request of level DEBUG and INFO issued to the "chapter3.MyApp2"and "chapter3.Foo" loggers will be suppressed. Running the *MyApp2* application with *sample2.properties* configuration file will produce no output.

Changing the level of the "chapter3" logger to INFO will suppress DEBUG messages but will allow messages of level INFO and above. Altering *sample2.properties* to

```
log4j.logger.chapter3=INFO
```

and running the *MyApp2* application with this modified configuration script will yield:

```
[main] INFO   chapter3.MyApp2 - Entering application.
[main] INFO   chapter3.MyApp2 - Exiting application.
```

Needless to say, one can configure the levels of as many loggers as one wishes. In the next configuration file we set the level of the "chapter3" logger to WARN but at the same time set the level of the "chapter3.Foo" logger to DEBUG.

Example 3-7: Setting the levels of multiple loggers (examples/chapter3/sample3.properties)

```
log4j.rootLogger=DEBUG, CON
log4j.appender.CON=org.apache.log4j.ConsoleAppender
log4j.appender.CON.layout=org.apache.log4j.PatternLayout

log4j.appender.CON.layout.ConversionPattern=%d %-5p %c - %m%n

# Allow requests level WARN or above in "chapter3" package except in
# "chapter3.Foo" where DEBUG or above is allowed.

log4j.logger.chapter3=WARN
log4j.logger.chapter3.Foo=DEBUG
```

Running *MyApp2* with this configuration file will result in the following output on the console, except the date that will be different for obvious reasons.

```
2002-03-20 16:36:36,069 DEBUG chapter3.Foo - Did it again!
```

After `PropertyConfigurator` configures log4j using the *sample3.properties* file, the logger settings, more specifically their levels, are summarized in the following table.

Logger name	Assigned level	Effective level
root	DEBUG	DEBUG
chapter3	WARN	WARN
chapter3.MyApp2	null	WARN
chapter3.Foo	DEBUG	DEBUG

It follows that the two logging statements of level `INFO` in the *MyApp2* class are suppressed while the debug statement in `Foo.doIt()` method prints without hindrance. Note that the level of the root logger is always set to a non-null value, which is `DEBUG` by default.

> The logger-level filter depends on effective level of the logger being invoked, *not* the effective level of any parent loggers where appenders are attached.

One rather important point to remember is that the logger-level filter depends on effective level of the logger being invoked, *not* the effective level of any parent loggers where appenders are attached. The configuration file *sample4.properties* is a case in point:

Example 3-8 Independence of level settings (examples/chapter3/sample4.properties)

```
# We set the level of the root logger to OFF.
log4j.rootLogger=OFF, CON
log4j.appender.CON=org.apache.log4j.ConsoleAppender
log4j.appender.CON.layout=org.apache.log4j.PatternLayout

log4j.appender.CON.layout.ConversionPattern=%d %-5p %c - %m%n

# Set the level of the chapter3 logger to DEBUG.
log4j.logger.chapter3=DEBUG
```

The following table lists the loggers and their assigned and effective levels after configuration with the *sample4.properties* configuration script.

Logger name	Assigned level	Effective level
Root	OFF	OFF
chapter3	DEBUG	DEBUG
chapter3.MyApp2	null	DEBUG
chapter3.Foo	null	DEBUG

The root logger is turned off totally, yet running *MyApp2* with *sample4.properties* will output:

```
2002-03-20 19:39:02,239 INFO  chapter3.MyApp2 - Entering application.
2002-03-20 19:39:02,249 DEBUG chapter3.Foo - Did it again!
2002-03-20 19:39:02,249 INFO  chapter3.MyApp2 - Exiting application.
```

Thus, the effective level of the root logger had no effect because the loggers in `chapter3.MyApp2` and `chapter3.Foo` classes inherit their level from the "chapter3" logger. This result is a straigtforward application of the rules announced so far. As logical as it is, it is a common log4j pitfall that many novice users fall into.

Setting the threshold of an Appender

It is possible to restrain the contents of a log file (or any output target) by level. All appenders shipped with the log4j distribution extend `AppenderSkeleton` class which admits a property called **Threshold**. Setting the **Threshold** option of an appender will filter out all log events with a level lower than the level of the threshold.

For example, setting the threshold of an appender to `DEBUG` will let `INFO`, `WARN`, `ERROR` and `FATAL` messages to log, along with `DEBUG` messages. This is usually acceptable as there is little use for `DEBUG` messages without the surrounding `INFO`, `WARN`, `ERROR` and `FATAL` messages. In a similar vein, setting the threshold to `ER-ROR` will filter out `DEBUG`, `INFO` and `WARN` messages but will not hinder `ERROR` and `FATAL` messages. This policy usually best encapsulates what the user actually wants to do, as opposed to her mind-projected solution.

The configuration file *sample5.properties* shows an example of setting an appender specific threshold.

Example 3-9:Setting appender specific threshold (examples/chapter3/sample5.properties)

```
log4j.rootLogger=DEBUG, C
log4j.appender.C=org.apache.log4j.ConsoleAppender

# Set the appender threshold to INFO
log4j.appender.C.Threshold=INFO
log4j.appender.C.layout=org.apache.log4j.PatternLayout
log4j.appender.C.layout.ConversionPattern=%-4r [%t] %-5p %c %x - %m%n
```

Running *MyApp2* with this configuration script will yield the following output:

```
0    [main] INFO  chapter3.MyApp2  - Entering application.
10   [main] INFO  chapter3.MyApp2  - Exiting application.
```

Since the debug request to the "chapter3.Foo" logger is below the threshold of the appender named C, it is dropped by that appender. Note that as far as the loggers are concerned the log message was enabled; it is the appender which decided to drop the message at the last minute.

If you must absolutely filter events by exact level match, then you can attach a LevelMatchFilter to a given appender in order to filter out logging events by exact level match. The LevelMatchFilter is an instance of a custom filter. Custom filters are discussed in Chapter 6. Note that PropertyConfigurator does not support custom filters which can only be specified in configuration scripts expressed in XML format.

Multiple appenders

As mentioned in the previous chapter, log4j allows attaching multiple appenders to any logger. The next configuration script illustrates the configuration of multiple appenders.

Example 3-10: Multiple appenders (examples/chapter3/multiple.properties)

```
log4j.rootLogger=debug, stdout, R

log4j.appender.stdout=org.apache.log4j.ConsoleAppender
log4j.appender.stdout.layout=org.apache.log4j.PatternLayout

# Pattern to output the caller's file name and line number.
log4j.appender.stdout.layout.ConversionPattern=%5p [%t] (%F:%L) - %m%n

log4j.appender.R=org.apache.log4j.RollingFileAppender
log4j.appender.R.File=example.log

log4j.appender.R.MaxFileSize=100KB
# Keep one backup file
log4j.appender.R.MaxBackupIndex=1

log4j.appender.R.layout=org.apache.log4j.PatternLayout
log4j.appender.R.layout.ConversionPattern=%p %t %c - %m%n
```

The above script begins by configuring a ConsoleAppender and then a RollingFileAppender. These appenders are respectively called stdout and R. The PatternLayout instance associated with stdout (the ConsoleAppender) is instructed to extract the file name and the line number of the logging request by virtue of the %F and %L conversion specifiers. Running *MyApp2* with this configuration file will output the following on the console.

```
 INFO [main] (MyApp2.java:15) - Entering application.
DEBUG [main] (Foo.java:8) - Did it again!
 INFO [main] (MyApp2.java:18) - Exiting application.
```

In addition, note that a second appender named R, has been attached to the root logger. Thus, output will also be directed to the *example.log* file, the target of the RollingFileAppender named R. This file will be rolled over when it reaches 100KB. When rollover occurs, the old version of *example.log* is automatically moved to *example.log.1*. The RollingFileAppender will be covered later in the book.

Novice log4j users tend to forget that appenders are cumulative. *By default, a logger will log to the appenders attached to itself (if there are any) as well as all the appenders attached to its ancestors.* Thus, attaching the same appender to multiple loggers will cause logging output to be duplicated.

Example 3-11:Duplicate appenders (examples/chapter3/duplicate.properties)

```
log4j.debug=true
log4j.rootLogger=debug, CON
log4j.appender.CON=org.apache.log4j.ConsoleAppender
log4j.appender.CON.layout=org.apache.log4j.PatternLayout
log4j.appender.CON.layout.ConversionPattern=%r %p %t %c - %m%n

# The CON appender is also attached to the "chapter3" logger. The
# following directive does not set the level of "chapter3" logger by
# leaving its level field empty.
log4j.logger.chapter3=,CON
```

Running *MyApp2* with *duplicate.properties* will yield the following output.

```
log4j: Parsing for [root] with value=[debug, CON].
log4j: Level token is [debug].
log4j: Category root set to DEBUG
log4j: Parsing appender named "CON".
log4j: Parsing layout options for "CON".
log4j: Setting property [conversionPattern] to [%r %p %t %c - %m%n].
log4j: End of parsing for "CON".
log4j: Parsed "CON" options.
log4j: Parsing for [chapter3] with value=[,CON].
log4j: Parsing appender named "CON".
log4j: Appender "CON" was already parsed.
log4j: Handling log4j.additivity.chapter3=[null]
log4j: Finished configuring.
0 INFO main chapter3.MyApp2 - Entering application.
0 INFO main chapter3.MyApp2 - Entering application.
0 DEBUG main chapter3.Foo - Did it again!
0 DEBUG main chapter3.Foo - Did it again!
0 INFO main chapter3.MyApp2 - Exiting application.
0 INFO main chapter3.MyApp2 - Exiting application.
```

Notice the duplicated output. The appender named CON is attached to two loggers: to root and to "chapter3". Since the root logger is the ancestor of all loggers and "chapter3" is the parent of "chapter3.MyApp2" and "chapter3.Foo", logging request made with the latter two will be written twice, once because CON is attached to "chapter3" and once because it is attached to the root logger.

Assuredly, the purpose of appender additivity is not to confuse for new users. It is a quite handy log4j feature. For instance, one can configure logging such that only log messages above a certain threshold level appear on the console (for all loggers in the system) while messages only from some specific set of loggers flow into a specific appender.

Example 3-12: Better use of multiple appenders (examples/chapter3/restricted.properties)

```
log4j.debug=true
log4j.appender.CON=org.apache.log4j.ConsoleAppender
log4j.appender.CON.Threshold=INFO
log4j.appender.CON.layout=org.apache.log4j.PatternLayout
log4j.appender.CON.layout.ConversionPattern=%r %p [%t] %c - %m%n

log4j.appender.CH3=org.apache.log4j.FileAppender
log4j.appender.CH3.File=ch3restricted.log
log4j.appender.CH3.layout=org.apache.log4j.PatternLayout
log4j.appender.CH3.layout.ConversionPattern=%r %p %t %c - %m%n

log4j.rootLogger=debug, CON
log4j.logger.chapter3=INHERITED,CH3
```

In this example, the appender named CON will drop events below the INFO level because its threshold is set to INFO. As this appender is attached to the root logger and by virtue of the appender additivity rule, it will service the events generated by all loggers in the hierarchy, which are all placed below root by construction. The FileAppender named CH3 will direct its output to the file *ch3restricted.log* in the current directory. The CH3 appender is attached to the "chapter3" logger. For extra emphasis, the "chapter3" logger has its level explicitly set to INHERITED or NULL which means that it will inherit its level from higher in the hierarchy. Given that all non-root loggers have their level set to null by default, setting the level of the "chapter3" was not strictly necessary. To summarize, the console appender will log messages of level INFO and above (for *all loggers* in the system) whereas only logging events (of *all levels*) from under "chapter3" tree go into a file named *ch3restricted.log*.

Overriding the default cumulative behavior

In case the default cumulative behavior turns out to be unsuitable for one's needs, one can override it by setting the additivity flag to false. Thus, a branch in your logger tree may direct output to a set of appenders different than those in the rest of the tree.

Example 3-13: Setting the additivity flag (examples/chapter3/additivityFlag.properties)

```
# This configuration script shows the usage of the additivity
# flag of a logger in conjunction with multiple appenders.

log4j.rootLogger=debug, STDOUT

log4j.appender.STDOUT=org.apache.log4j.ConsoleAppender
log4j.appender.STDOUT.layout=org.apache.log4j.PatternLayout
log4j.appender.STDOUT.layout.ConversionPattern=%p %t %c - %m%n

log4j.appender.FOO=org.apache.log4j.FileAppender
log4j.appender.FOO.File=foo.log
log4j.appender.FOO.layout=org.apache.log4j.PatternLayout
log4j.appender.FOO.layout.ConversionPattern=%d %p %t %c - %m%n

# Attach the FOO appender to chapter3.Foo logger
log4j.logger.chapter3.Foo=null, FOO
# Set the additivity flag of "chapter3.Foo" to false
log4j.additivity.chapter3.Foo=false
```

In this example, the appender named FOO is attached to the "chapter3.Foo" logger. Moreover, the "chapter3.Foo" logger has its additivity flag set to false such that its logging output will be sent to the appender named FOO but not to any appender attached higher in the hierarchy. Other loggers remain oblivious to the additivity setting of the "chapter3.Foo" logger. Running the *MyApp2* application with the *additivityFlag.properties* configuration file will output results on the console from the "chapter3.MyApp2" logger. However, output from the "chapter3.Foo" logger will appear in the *foo.log* file and only in that file.

To obtain these different logging behaviors we did not need to recompile any code. For example, we could just as easily have logged to a UNIX Syslog daemon, redirected output from the chapter3.Foo class and only from that class to an NT Event logger, or forwarded logging events to a remote log4j server, which would log according to local server policy, possibly by forwarding the log event to yet another log4j server. Configuration scripts in property format (key=value) are quite easy to write. Parsing them requires log4j and obviously the JDK. Configuration files in XML format, which we are about to present, additionally require the presence of a JAXP compatible XML parser. In exchange, they permit the representation of more elaborate and powerful log4j configurations.

Configuration files in XML

As mentioned previously, log4j also supports configuration files written in XML format. These configuration files are parsed by the org.apache.log4j.-

xml.DOMConfigurator. The *MyApp3* application listed next uses the DOMCon-figurator.

```
package chapter3;
import org.apache.log4j.Logger;
import org.apache.log4j.xml.DOMConfigurator;

public class MyApp3 {
  final static Logger logger = Logger.getLogger(MyApp3.class);

  public static void main(String[] args) {
    DOMConfigurator.configure(args[0]);

    logger.info("Entering application.");
    Foo foo = new Foo();
    foo.doIt();
    logger.info("Exiting application.");
  }
}
```

Notice the similarity of invoking the DOMConfigurator to invoking Property-Configurator. The compilation *MyApp3.java* requires the presence of the JAXP classes on the CLASSPATH. The execution of all the DOMConfigurator related examples require the presence of a JAXP compatible parser, e.g. *crimson.jar* or *xerces.jar*. The partitioning of jar files into the abstract JAXP API and its imple-menting parser depend on the parser family, e.g. crimson, Xerces, Xerces2, and also on the exact version of the parser within the same family. Consult the docu-mentation accompanying your JAXP compatible parser for details.

Before discussing the syntax of XML configuration files, below is an example that configures log4j in the same as BasicConfigurator.configure() method or the *sample0.properties* script we have seen earlier, in conjunction with Property-Configurator.

Example 3-14: BasicConfigurator.configure() equivalent (examples/chapter3/sample0.xml)

```
<?xml version="1.0" encoding="UTF-8" ?>
<!DOCTYPE log4j:configuration SYSTEM "log4j.dtd">

<log4j:configuration xmlns:log4j='http://jakarta.apache.org/log4j/'>

  <appender name="STDOUT" class="org.apache.log4j.ConsoleAppender">
    <layout class="org.apache.log4j.PatternLayout">
      <param name="ConversionPattern"
             value="%-4r [%t] %-5p %c %x - %m%n"/>
    </layout>
  </appender>
```

```
<root>
  <level value="debug"/>
  <appender-ref ref="STDOUT"/>
</root>
</log4j:configuration>
```

The above configuration script is available as *sample0.xml* under the *examples/chapter3* directory. After ensuring that the current directory is *LOG4J_MANUAL/examples*, try executing the following command:

```
java chapter3.MyApp3 chapter3/sample0.xml
```

The output of this command is very similar to the output of *MyApp1*, except that *MyApp3* application references a logger called "chapter3.MyApp3" instead of "chapter3.MyApp1". The output will reflect this difference.

You can instruct log4j to output internal debugging messages on the console. This is accomplished by the debug attribute within the `<log4j:configuration>` element. As in:

```
<log4j:configuration debug="true"
                     xmlns:log4j='http://jakarta.apache.org/log4j/'>
  ...
</log4j:configuration>
```

As surprising as it may seem, the *log4j.dtd* does not need to be placed in the same directory as the XML file. In fact, it does not need to be placed anywhere. The *log4j.dtd* is extracted from *log4j.jar* and handed to the XML parser. If you are interested in the details, this is accomplished by setting the systemID in the InputSource[13] object that is passed to the parse method of a valid `DocumentBuilder`[14] instance.

Syntax of XML scripts

The syntax of XML scripts is specified by the *log4j.dtd*. In case of doubt, it remains the ultimate authority regarding the correct syntax. Instead of an unsavory listing of the *log4j.dtd*, we choose to present a more amenable and narrative description here. The information you expect to find in XML script is similar to the information found key/value scripts. Obviously, a configuration file written in XML, as all XML documents, must be well-formed. While reading the following

---

[13] `InputSource` class is part of the `org.xml.sax` package.

[14] `DocumentBuilder` class is part of the `javax.xml.parsers` package of the JAXP API.

syntax description, I encourage you to compare it with the examples found in *sample0.xml* presented above, as well other XML configuration scripts supplied with this manual. The next few pages present the elements recognized by the `DOMConfigurator`. These elements are listed in a flat style without any form of rigid nesting.

- `<log4j:configuration>` element:

The document root in for log4j scripts is the `<log4j:configuration>` element which is declared to be in the *http://jakarta.apache.org/log4j/* namespace. This element contains zero or more `<renderer>` elements, zero or more `<appender>` elements, zero or more `<logger>` elements and at most one `<root>` element, in that order, as summarized in Figure 3-2 below.

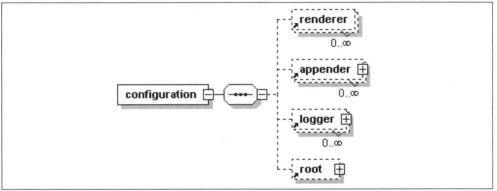

Figure 3-2. The `<log4j:configuration>` element and its children.

The `<log4j:configuration>` element admits two attributes: *threshold* and *debug*. The *threshold* attribute can take the case insensitive string values "all", "debug", info", "warn", "error", "fatal", and "off". As the name indicates, it sets the value of the hierarchy-wide threshold. If unspecified, the hierarchy-wide threshold keeps its existing value which is `Level.ALL` by default. The *debug* attribute can take the values "true" or "false". This attribute controls the internal logging feature of log4j.

The children of the `<log4j:configuration>` element are discussed next.

- `<renderer>` element:

    This element is empty; it has neither children nor body. However, it must contain two attributes: *renderedClass* and *renderingClass* both of which are required.

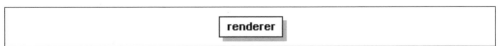

Figure 3-3: The `<renderer>` element.

A sample configuration file *objectRendering.xml* can be found under the *examples/chapter3/* directory. See also the source files *ObjectRenderingSample.java, Fruit.java* and *Orange.java* in the same directory for a complete example.

- `<appender>` element:

  This element admits two attributes `name` and `class` both of which are mandatory. The `name` attribute specifies the name of the appender whereas the `class` attribute specifies the fully qualified name of the class of which the named appender will be an instance. The appender element contains zero or one `<errorHandler>` elements, followed by zero or more `<param>` elements, followed by zero or one `<layout>` elements, followed by zero or more `<filter>` elements, and lastly zero or more `<appender-ref>` elements, as illustrated in Figure 3-4 below.

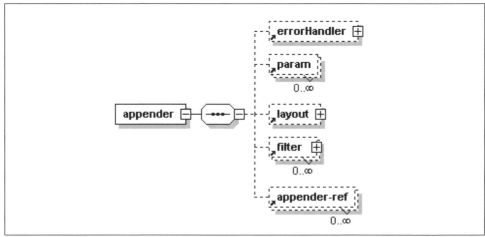

Figure 3-4. The `<appender>` element and its children.

- `<errorHandler>` element:

  Each appender has an associated error handler to respond its error conditions. Error handlers will be discussed in the next chapter. The present description is limited to the syntax of the `<errorHandler>` element. The `<errorHandler>` element admits a mandatory `class` attribute which corresponds to the fully qualified name of the error handler implementation to instantiate. It also contains zero or more `<param>` elements, followed by at most one `<root-ref>` element, followed by zero or more `<logger-ref>` elements, and lastly zero or more `<appender-ref>` elements, as illustrated in Figure 3-5 below.

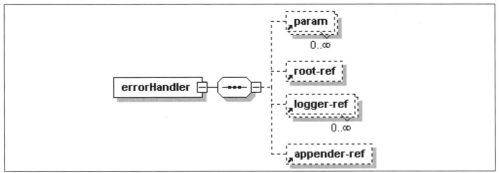

Figure 3-5: The <errorHandler> element and its children.

The <root-ref> and <logger-ref> elements indicate the loggers where the containing appender is attached to. The <appender-ref> element is a reference to a secondary appender that can be used as a fallback appender when the primary appender, i.e. the containing appender, fails.

- **<param>** element:

  The <param> element appears as a child in a number of other elements such as <appender>, <layout> and <filter>. It admits no child elements but takes two mandatory attributes: *name* and *value*, which correspond to the property name and value to set in the object associated with the parent element.

  The *options*, a.k.a. *properties*, of appenders, layouts or filters are inferred dynamically using standard JavaBeans conventions. Any setter method taking a single primitive java type, an Integer, a Long, a String or a Boolean parameter implies an option name. For example, given that the FileAppender class contains setAppend(boolean), setBufferSize(int) and setFile(String) as member methods, then it follows that **Append**, **BufferSize** and **File** are all valid option names. Log4j can also deal with setter methods taking an org.apache.log4j.Level parameter. For example, since the AppenderSkeleton class[15] has setThreshold(Level) as a member method, **Threshold** is a valid option for all log4j appenders extending the AppenderSkeleton class.

---

[15] The AppenderSkeleton class is the base class for all appenders shipped in the official log4j distribution.

- **`<layout>`** element:

  The `<layout>` element takes a mandatory *class* attribute specifying the fully qualified name of the class of which the associated layout should be an instance. It can have zero or more `<param>` elements as children. Similar to the `<param>` elements contained in `<appender>` elements, the `<param>` elements in `<layout>` element are interpreted as options for the layout instance.

Figure 3-6: The <layout> element and its children.

- **`<filter>`** element:

Zero or more filters can be attached to any appender. Filters will be discussed in later chapters. The structure of a `<filter>` element is identical to the structure of a `<layout>` element. The `<filter>` element takes a *class* attribute and contains one or more `<param>` elements as children.

Figure 3-7: The <filter> element.

- **`<appender-ref>`** element:

This element allows referring to another appender by name. It admits the *ref* attribute which should match the name of an appender declared elsewhere within an `<appender>` element. The `<appender-ref>` element does not contain children.

Figure 3-8: The <appender-ref> element.

- **`<logger>`** element:

  The `<logger>` element configures `Logger` instances. It takes exactly one mandatory *name* attribute and an optional *additivity* attribute, which take values "true" or "false". The `<logger>` element admits at most one `<level>` element which is discussed next. The `<logger>` element may contain zero or more `<appender-ref>` elements; each appender thus referenced is added to the named logger. It is important to keep mind that each named logger that is declared with a <logger> element first has all its appenders removed and only then are the referenced appenders attached to it. In particular, if there are no appender references, then the named logger will lose all its appenders.

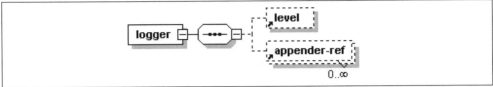

Figure 3-9: The <logger> element and its children.

- **<level>** element:

  The <level> element is used to set logger levels. It admits two attributes *value* and *class*. The value attribute can be one of the strings "DEBUG", "INFO", WARN" "ERROR" or "FATAL". The special case-insensitive value "INHERITED", or its synonym "NULL", will force the level of the logger to be inherited from higher up in the hierarchy. Note that the level of the root logger cannot be inherited. If you set the level of a logger and later decide that it should inherit its level, then you need to specify "INHERITED" or its synonym "NULL" as the level value. The *class* attribute allows you to specify a custom level where the value of the attribute is the fully qualified name of a custom level class. You may alternatively use the "level#classname" syntax within the *value* attribute. The <level> element has no children.

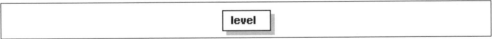

Figure 3-10: The <level> element.

- **<root>** element:

  The <root> element configures the root logger. It does not admit any attributes because the additivity flag does not apply to the root logger. Moreover, since the root logger cannot be named, it does not admit a *name* attribute either. The <root> element admits at most one <level> element and zero or more <appender-ref> elements. Similar to the <logger> element, declaring a <root> element will have the effect of first closing and then detaching all its current appenders and only subsequently will referenced appenders, if any, will be added. In particular, if it has no appender references, then the root logger will lose all its appenders.

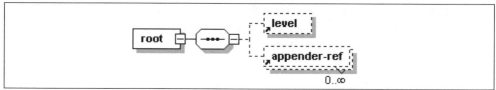

Figure 3-11: The <root> element:

Putting all the previous elements together we get:

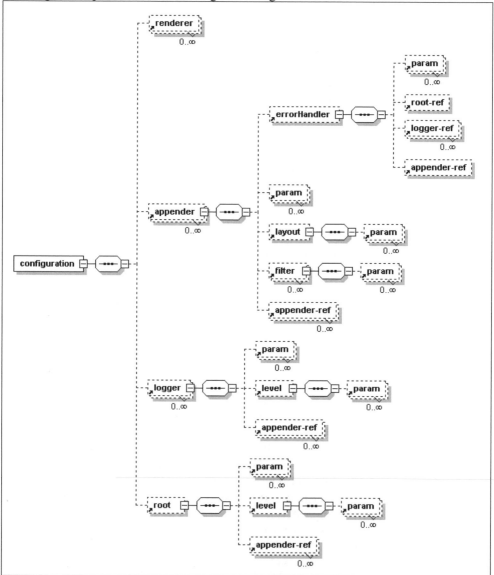

Figure 3-12: A summary of all the elements in a log4j configuration script.

Setting a hierarchy-wide threshold (XML)

As mentioned previously, the fastest but also the least flexible way of filtering logging statements is by setting a hierarchy-wide threshold. It is quite straightforward to set the hierarchy-wide threshold, a.k.a. repository-wide threshold, in an XML configuration script. This is illustrated in the sample configuration file *sample1.xml* listed below. This file is also available under the *examples/chapter3/* directory.

Example 3-15:Setting a hierarchy-wide threshold (examples/chapter3/sample1.xml)

```xml
<?xml version="1.0" encoding="UTF-8" ?>
<!DOCTYPE log4j:configuration SYSTEM "log4j.dtd">

<log4j:configuration threshold="warn"
                     xmlns:log4j='http://jakarta.apache.org/log4j/'>

  <appender name="STDOUT" class="org.apache.log4j.ConsoleAppender">
    <layout class="org.apache.log4j.SimpleLayout"/>
  </appender>

  <root>
    <appender-ref ref="STDOUT" />
  </root>
</log4j:configuration>
```

The above configuration file sets the hierarchy-wide threshold to warn. It then creates a `ConsoleAppender` called "STDOUT" associating it with a `SimpleLayout`. "STDOUT" is then added to the root logger. Note that the root logger has its level set to DEBUG by default. In the absence of other instructions, the level of the root logger, that is DEBUG in this particular case, will be inherited by all other loggers. Given that the hierarchy-wide threshold is set to level WARN and that *MyApp3* does not contain any warn(), error() or fatal() log statements, running the *MyApp3* application with the *sample1.xml* configuration script will not produce any logging output.

Setting the level of a logger (XML)

The contents of this section are very similar to the contents of previous section of the same name describing configuration files in properties format. The major difference is that it employs XML syntax instead of key=value syntax.

Setting the level of a logger is as simple as declaring it and setting its level, as the next example illustrates. Suppose we are no longer interested in seeing any INFO or DEBUG level logs from any component belonging to the chapter3 package. The following configuration file, available digitally as *examples/chapter/sample2.xml*, shows how to achieve that.

Example 3-16: Setting the level of a logger (examples/chapter3/sample2.xml)

```
<?xml version="1.0" encoding="UTF-8" ?>
<!DOCTYPE log4j:configuration SYSTEM "log4j.dtd">

<log4j:configuration xmlns:log4j='http://jakarta.apache.org/log4j/'>

  <appender name="STDOUT" class="org.apache.log4j.ConsoleAppender">
    <layout class="org.apache.log4j.PatternLayout">
      <param name="ConversionPattern" value="[%t] %-5p %c - %m%n"/>
    </layout>
  </appender>

  <logger name="chapter3">
    <level value="OFF"/>
  </logger>

  <root>
    <!-- The following level element is not necessary since the -->
    <!-- level of the root level is set to DEBUG by default.    -->
    <level value="debug"/>
    <appender-ref ref="STDOUT" />
  </root>
</log4j:configuration>
```

This configuration file sets the level of the logger named "chapter3"to OFF. This logger is the parent of the "chapter3.MyApp3" and "chapter3.Foo" loggers. As such, these loggers will inherit the OFF level. Consequently, log requests of all levels, including of level DEBUG and INFO, made to these loggers will be suppressed. In other words, running the *MyApp3* application with configuration file *sample2.xml* will produce no output at all.

Changing the level of the "chapter3" logger to INFO will suppress DEBUG messages but will allow INFO messages. Altering *sample2.xml* to

```
<logger name="chapter3">
  <level value="INFO"/>
</logger>
```

will yield:

```
[main] INFO  chapter3.MyApp3 - Entering application.
[main] INFO  chapter3.MyApp3 - Exiting application.
```

Obviously, you can configure the levels of as many loggers as you wish. In the
next configuration file we set the level of the "chapter3" logger to INFO but at the
same time set the level of the "chapter3.Foo" logger to DEBUG.

Example 3-17: Setting the level of multiple loggers (examples/chapter3/sample3.xml)

```
<?xml version="1.0" encoding="UTF-8" ?>
<!DOCTYPE log4j:configuration SYSTEM "log4j.dtd">

<log4j:configuration xmlns:log4j='http://jakarta.apache.org/log4j/'>

   <appender name="STDOUT" class="org.apache.log4j.ConsoleAppender">
      <layout class="org.apache.log4j.PatternLayout">
         <param name="ConversionPattern" value="%d %5p %c - %m%n"/>
      </layout>
   </appender>

   <logger name="chapter3">
      <level value="INFO"/>
   </logger>

   <logger name="chapter3.Foo">
      <level value="DEBUG"/>
   </logger>

   <root>
      <level value="debug"/>
      <appender-ref ref="STDOUT" />
   </root>
</log4j:configuration>
```

Running *MyAp3* with this configuration file will result in the following output on
the console. (The date will be different for obvious reasons.)

```
2002-05-16 23:51:51,893  INFO chapter3.MyApp3 - Entering application.
2002-05-16 23:51:51,893 DEBUG chapter3.Foo - Did it again!
2002-05-16 23:51:51,893  INFO chapter3.MyApp3 - Exiting application.
```

After DOMConfigurator configures log4j using the *sample3.xml* file, the logger
settings, more specifically their levels, are summarized in the following table.

Logger name	Assigned level	Effective level
root	DEBUG	DEBUG
chapter3	INFO	INFO
chapter3.MyApp2	null	INFO
chapter3.Foo	DEBUG	DEBUG

It follows that the two logging statements of level INFO in the *MyAp3* class are enabled while the debug statement in Foo.doIt() method will also print without
hindrance. Note that the level of the root logger is always set to a non-null value,
which is DEBUG by default. One rather important point to remember is that the

logger-level filter depends on the effective level of the logger being invoked, not the level of the logger where the appenders are attached. The configuration file *sample4.xml* is a case in point:

Example 3-18: 3-19 Independence of level settings (examples/chapter3/sample4.xml)

```
<?xml version="1.0" encoding="UTF-8" ?>
<!DOCTYPE log4j:configuration SYSTEM "log4j.dtd">

<log4j:configuration xmlns:log4j='http://jakarta.apache.org/log4j/'>

  <appender name="STDOUT" class="org.apache.log4j.ConsoleAppender">
    <layout class="org.apache.log4j.PatternLayout">
      <param name="ConversionPattern" value="%p %c - %m%n"/>
    </layout>
  </appender>

  <logger name="chapter3">
    <level value="INFO"/>
  </logger>

  <root>
    <level value="OFF"/>
    <appender-ref ref="STDOUT" />
  </root>
</log4j:configuration>
```

The following table lists the loggers and their level setting after applying the *sample4.xml* configuration file.

Logger name	Assigned level	Effective level
Root	OFF	OFF
chapter3	INFO	INFO
chapter3.MyApp2	null	INFO
chapter3.Foo	null	INFO

The `ConsoleAppender` named "STDOUT," the only configured appender in *sample4.xml*, is attached to the root logger whose level is set to OFF. However, running *MyApp3* with configuration script *sample4.xml* will output:

```
INFO chapter3.MyApp3 - Entering application.
INFO chapter3.MyApp3 - Exiting application.
```

Thus, the level of the root logger has no apparent effect because the loggers in `chapter3.MyApp3` and `chapter3.Foo` classes, namely "chapter3.MyApp3" and "chapter3.Foo", inherit their level from the "chapter3" logger which has its level set to INFO. As noted previously, the "chapter3" logger exists by virtue of its declaration in the configuration file – even if the Java source code does not directly refer to it.

Setting the threshold of an Appender (XML)

It is possible to limit the output of an appender by level. All appenders shipped with the log4j distribution extend the `AppenderSkeleton` class which admits a property called **Threshold**. Setting the **Threshold** option of an appender will filter out all log events with a level lower than the level of the threshold. For example, setting the threshold of an appender to `INFO` will filter out `DEBUG` messages but will allow `WARN`, `ERROR` and `FATAL` messages to pass, along with `INFO` messages. This is usually acceptable as there is little use for `INFO` messages without the surrounding `WARN`, `ERROR` and `FATAL` messages. In a similar vein, setting the threshold of an appender to `ERROR` will filter out `DEBUG`, `INFO` and `WARN` messages but not `ERROR` or `FATAL` messages. The configuration file *sample5.xml* gives an example for setting the appender threshold.

Example 3-20: Setting the threshold of an appender (examples/chapter3/sample5.xml)

```
<?xml version="1.0" encoding="UTF-8" ?>
<!DOCTYPE log4j:configuration SYSTEM "log4j.dtd">

<log4j:configuration xmlns:log4j='http://jakarta.apache.org/log4j/'>

  <appender name="CONSOLE" class="org.apache.log4j.ConsoleAppender">
    <param name="Threshold" value="INFO"/>
    <layout class="org.apache.log4j.PatternLayout">
      <param name="ConversionPattern" value="%-5p [%t] %c - %m%n"/>
    </layout>
  </appender>

  <root>
    <level value="debug" />
    <appender-ref ref="CONSOLE" />
  </root>
</log4j:configuration>
```

Running *MyAp3* with the *sample5.xml* configuration scripts yields:

```
INFO  [main] chapter3.MyApp3 - Entering application.
INFO  [main] chapter3.MyApp3 - Exiting application.
```

Note that since the debug request in the `Foo.doIt()` method is below the threshold of the CONSOLE appender, it is dropped by that appender. Note that as far as the logger named "chapter3.Foo" is concerned the log message was enabled. It is the appender which decided to drop the message at the last minute.

If you must absolutely filter events by exact level match, then you can attach a
`LevelMatchFilter` to a given appender in order to filter out logging events by
exact level match. The `LevelMatchFilter` is an instance of a custom filter as
discussed in Chapter 6.

Multiple Appenders (XML)

Logging to multiple appenders is as easy as defining the various appenders and
referencing them in a logger, as the next configuration file illustrates:

Example 3-21: Defining multiple appenders (examples/chapter3/multiple.xml)

```xml
<?xml version="1.0" encoding="UTF-8" ?>
<!DOCTYPE log4j:configuration SYSTEM "log4j.dtd">

<log4j:configuration debug="true"
xmlns:log4j='http://jakarta.apache.org/log4j/'>

   <appender name="LIFE_CYCLE" class="org.apache.log4j.FileAppender">
     <param name="File" value="lifecyle.log"/>
     <param name="Threshold" value="INFO"/>
     <layout class="org.apache.log4j.PatternLayout">
       <param name="ConversionPattern"
             value="%d %5p [%t] %c (%F:%L) - %m%n"/>
     </layout>
   </appender>

   <appender name="ROLLING"
             class="org.apache.log4j.RollingFileAppender">
     <param name="File" value="sample.log"/>
     <param name="MaxFileSize" value="100KB"/>
     <param name="MaxBackupIndex" value="2"/>
     <layout class="org.apache.log4j.PatternLayout">
       <param name="ConversionPattern" value="%m%n"/>
     </layout>
   </appender>

   <root>
     <appender-ref ref="LIFE_CYCLE" />
     <appender-ref ref="ROLLING" />
   </root>
</log4j:configuration>
```

This configuration scripts defines two appenders called LIFE_CYCLE and ROLL-
ING. The LIFE_CYCLE appender logs to a file called *lifecycle.log*. It has its
Threshold set to the INFO level such that DEBUG messages sent to this appender
will be dropped. The layout for this appender is a `PatternLayout` that outputs the
date, level (i.e. priority), thread name, logger name, file name and line number
where the log request is located, the message and line separator character(s). The

second appender called ROLLING outputs to a file called *sample.log* which will be rolled over when it reaches 100KB. The layout for this appender outputs only the message string followed by a line separator.

The appenders are attached to the root logger by referencing them by name within an `<appender-ref>` element. Note that each appender has its own layout. Layouts are usually not designed to be shared by multiple appenders. XML configuration files nor properties configuration scripts do not provide any syntactical means for sharing layouts.

 By default, appenders are cumulative: a logger will log to the appenders attached to itself (if any) as well as all the appenders attached to its ancestors.

New log4j users tend to forget that appenders are cumulative. By default, a logger will log to the appenders attached to itself (if any) as well as all the appenders attached to its ancestors. Thus, attaching the same appender to multiple loggers will cause logging output to be duplicated.

Example 3-22: Duplicate appenders (examples/chapter3/duplicate.xml)

```
<?xml version="1.0" encoding="UTF-8" ?>
<!DOCTYPE log4j:configuration SYSTEM "log4j.dtd">

<log4j:configuration debug="true"
xmlns:log4j='http://jakarta.apache.org/log4j/'>

  <appender name="CON" class="org.apache.log4j.ConsoleAppender">
    <layout class="org.apache.log4j.PatternLayout">
      <param name="ConversionPattern" value="%5p [%t] %c - %m%n"/>
    </layout>
  </appender>

  <logger name="chapter3">
    <appender-ref ref="CON" />
  </logger>

  <root>
    <level value="debug" />
    <appender-ref ref="CON" />
  </root>
</log4j:configuration>
```

Running *MyApp3* with *duplicate.xml* will yield the following output.

```
log4j: Threshold ="null".
log4j: Retreiving an instance of org.apache.log4j.Logger.
log4j: Setting [chapter3] additivity to [true].
```

```
log4j: Class name: [org.apache.log4j.ConsoleAppender]
log4j: Parsing layout of class: "org.apache.log4j.PatternLayout"
log4j: Setting property [conversionPattern] to [%5p [%t] %c - %m%n].
log4j: Adding appender named [CON] to category [chapter3].
log4j: Level value for root is  [debug].
log4j: root level set to DEBUG
log4j: Adding appender named [CON] to category [root].
 INFO [main] chapter3.MyApp3 - Entering application.
 INFO [main] chapter3.MyApp3 - Entering application.
DEBUG [main] chapter3.Foo - Did it again!
DEBUG [main] chapter3.Foo - Did it again!
 INFO [main] chapter3.MyApp3 - Exiting application.
 INFO [main] chapter3.MyApp3 - Exiting application.
```

Notice the duplicated output. The appender named CON is attached to two loggers, to root and to "chapter3". Since the root logger is the ancestor of all loggers and "chapter3" is the parent of "chapter3.MyApp2" and "chapter3.Foo", logging request made with these two loggers will be output twice, once because CON is attached to "chapter3" and once because it is attached to "root".

Appender additivity is not intended as a trap for new users. It is a quite convenient log4j feature. For instance, you can configure logging such that only log messages above a certain threshold appear on the console (for all loggers in the system) while messages only from some specific set of loggers flow into a specific appender.

Example 3-23: Better use of multiple appenders (examples/chapter3/restricted.properties)

```xml
<?xml version="1.0" encoding="UTF-8" ?>
<!DOCTYPE log4j:configuration SYSTEM "log4j.dtd">

<log4j:configuration debug="true"
                     xmlns:log4j='http://jakarta.apache.org/log4j/'>

  <appender name="CON" class="org.apache.log4j.ConsoleAppender">
    <param name="Threshold" value="INFO"/>
    <layout class="org.apache.log4j.PatternLayout">
      <param name="ConversionPattern" value="%5p [%t] %c - %m%n"/>
    </layout>
  </appender>

  <appender name="CH3" class="org.apache.log4j.FileAppender">
    <param name="File" value="ch3restricted.log"/>
    <layout class="org.apache.log4j.PatternLayout">
      <param name="ConversionPattern" value="%r %p %t %c - %m%n"/>
    </layout>
  </appender>
```

```
  <logger name="chapter3">
    <appender-ref ref="CH3" />
  </logger>

  <root>
    <lavel value="debug" />
    <appender-ref ref="CON" />
  </root>
</log4j:configuration>
```

In this example, the console appender will log messages of level INFO and above (for *all loggers* in the system) whereas only logs (of *all levels*) under the "chapter3" tree go into the *ch3restricted.log* file. As a more realistic example, the threshold of the CON appender would have been set to WARN as to restrict the console output to warnings and error messages.

Overriding the default cumulative behavior (XML)

In case the default cumulative behavior turns out to be unsuitable for one's needs, one can override it by setting the additivity flag to false. Thus, a branch in your logger tree may direct output to a set of appenders different than those of the rest of the tree.

Example 3-24: Setting the additivity flag (examples/chapter3/additivityFlag.xml)

```
<?xml version="1.0" encoding="UTF-8" ?>
<!DOCTYPE log4j:configuration SYSTEM "log4j.dtd">

<log4j:configuration debug="true"
              xmlns:log4j='http://jakarta.apache.org/log4j/'>
  <appender name="STDOUT"
           class="org.apache.log4j.ConsoleAppender">
    <param name="Threshold" value="INFO"/>
    <layout class="org.apache.log4j.PatternLayout">
      <param name="ConversionPattern" value="%p %t %c - %m%n"/>
    </layout>
  </appender>
  <appender name="FOO" class="org.apache.log4j.FileAppender">
    <param name="File" value="foo.log"/>
    <layout class="org.apache.log4j.PatternLayout">
      <param name="ConversionPattern" value="%p %t %c - %m%n"/>
    </layout>
  </appender>

  <logger name="chapter3.Foo" additivity="false">
    <appender-ref ref="FOO" />
  </logger>
```

```
<root>
  <level value="debug" />
  <appender-ref ref="STDOUT" />
</root>
</log4j:configuration>
```

This example, the appender named FOO is attached to the "chapter3.Foo" logger. Moreover, the "chapter3.Foo" logger has its additivity flag set to false such that its logging output will be sent to the appender named FOO but not to any appender attached higher in the hierarchy. Other loggers remain oblivious to the additivity setting of the "chapter3.Foo" logger. Running the *MyApp2* application with the *additivityFlag.properties* configuration file will output results on the console from the "chapter3.MyApp2" logger. However, output from the "chapter3.Foo" logger will appear in the *foo.log* file and only in that file.

Reloading configuration files

Reloading of a configuration file or reconfiguration of log4j from a different configuration file is allowed. It is also thread-safe. Contrary to expected behavior, during reconfiguration, log4j configurators do not reset the existing configuration. The rationale behind this somewhat unexpected behavior is to allow incremental changes to the configuration, as the next example illustrates.

Example 3-25: Initial configuration (examples/chapter3/initial.xml)

```
<?xml version="1.0" encoding="UTF-8" ?>
<!DOCTYPE log4j:configuration SYSTEM "log4j.dtd">
<log4j:configuration xmlns:log4j='http://jakarta.apache.org/log4j/'>
  <appender name="A1" class="org.apache.log4j.FileAppender">
    <param name="File" value="A1.log">
    <layout class="org.apache.log4j.PatternLayout">
      <param name="ConversionPattern" value="%d %p [%t] %c - %m%n"/>
    </layout>
  </appender>

  <appender name="A2" class="org.apache.log4j.FileAppender">
    <param name="File" value="A2.log">
    <layout class="org.apache.log4j.PatternLayout">
      <param name="ConversionPattern" value="%r %p [%t] %c - %m%n"/>
    </layout>
  </appender>

  <logger name="com.foo">
    <appender-ref ref="A2" />
  </logger>

  <logger name="com.wombat">
    <appender-ref ref="A2" />
  </logger>
```

```
  <root>
    <level value="debug" />
    <appender-ref ref="A1" />
  </root>
</log4j:configuration>
```

The *initial.xml* configuration file defines an appender A1 attached to the root logger, a second appender A2 is attached to loggers "com.foo" and "com.wombat".

The crucial point to remember is that invoking any of the log4j configurators does not reset the previous configuration. Reconfiguration has obviously some effect on the existing configuration. In particular, all appenders of any logger explicitly mentioned in the new configuration will be closed and removed from the logger. However, loggers which are not mentioned in the new configuration remain untouched. All the more, appenders attached to such loggers remain attached after reconfiguration.

For example, if an appender is attached to multiple loggers, it is possible for the appender to be closed during the reconfiguration but remain attached to a logger not mentioned in the second configuration file. If after reconfiguration you try to log to this closed appender, log4j will warn you about trying to log to a closed appender.

Example 3-26: Second configuration file

```
<?xml version="1.0" encoding="UTF-8" ?>
<!DOCTYPE log4j:configuration SYSTEM "log4j.dtd">

<log4j:configuration xmlns:log4j='http://jakarta.apache.org/log4j/'>
  <appender name="A1" class="org.apache.log4j.FileAppender">
    <param name="File" value="A1.log">
      <layout class="org.apache.log4j.PatternLayout">
        <param name="ConversionPattern" value="%r %p [%t] %c - %m%n"/>
      </layout>
  </appender>

  <logger name="com.foo">
    <level value="WARN">
  </logger>

  <root>
    <level value ="debug" />
    <appender-ref ref="A1" />
  </root>
</log4j:configuration>
```

When the second configuration file is read by the DOMConfigurator, since the root logger is mentioned in the second file, all the appenders in the root are closed and then removed. A new appender called A1 is then instantiated, configured and attached to root.

Logger "com.foo" is mentioned in the second configuration file. Consequently, A2 will be closed and removed from "com.foo". However, it will remain attached to com.wombat. Trying to log with "com.wombat" logger will cause log4j to emit a warning.

Embedded Libraries using log4j

In principle, configuring log4j is the responsibility of the end-user or generally the application deployer. Whenever possible, a library should not try to configure logging but leave it to the deployer. After all, logging output is useful only if someone will take the time to look at it. If the end-user wishes to log, then she should control the logging configuration. Nevertheless, it is helpful for the library developer to provide documentation on logging, preferably with complete working examples. The names of the loggers that the library uses are prime candidates to include in such documentation.

One rub with this policy, assuming the user does not configure log4j, is the dreaded warning message log4j outputs on the console on the first logging call in your library.

```
log4j:WARN No appenders could be found for logger (some.logger.name).
log4j:WARN Please initialize the log4j system properly.
```

We have already encountered this message in Chapter 1. It is log4j's way of letting you know that it is not been configured. As legitimate as it is, this message may unnecessarily alarm the end-user, inducing her to believe that there is an anomaly in your library or in the enclosing software being deployed.

Let Spookz Inc. be a company specialized in cryptographic software. The flagship product of Spookz Inc. is a purportedly unbreakable encryption algorithm packaged within their CryptoLib library. CryptoLib uses log4j for its logging. All loggers in CryptoLib are children of the "com.spookz.cryptolib" logger. In line with our policy of letting the end-user configure log4j, the engineers at Spookz decide to initially turn off all logging from within their library.

```
void turnOffCryptoLogging() {
  Logger.getInstance("com.spookz.cryptolib").setLevel(Level.OFF);
}
```

This method is invoked very early in the game before other code in CryptoLib has a chance to issue log requests. As long as the end-user does not configure log4j, all logging requests in cryptolib will be suppressed, including the worrisome "Please initialize log4j" warning message.

If on the contrary, the user decides to configure log4j, then there are two possible outcomes depending on the order of log4j configuration by the user and cryptolib turning off its logging.

If log4j configuration occurs *after* CryptoLib invokes `turnOffCryptoLog-ging()`, then the configuration established by the deployer will be determining. The user can easily turn on logging in CryptoLib, either programmatically or in a configuration script.

This can accomplished by including the following directive in a configuration file (properties format)

```
log4j.com.spookz.cryptolib=INHERITED
```

The same in XML is written as:

```
<logger name="com.spookz.cryptolib">
    <level name="INHERITED"/>
</logger>
```

These directives set the level of the "com.spookz.cryptolib" logger to `null` causing it and its children to inherit their level from higher up in the logger hierarchy. The deployer obviously has the possibility to configure the "com.spookz.cryptolib" logger in different ways, as with any other logger.

In a less favorable turn of events, log4j configuration by the user can occur *before* `turnOffCryptoLogging` method is called. In this case, CryptoLib effectively overrides the deployer's intended logging configuration. This outcome is likely to occasion some confusion and construed as being unfriendly. Fortunately, we can avoid this undesired interference with a small modification to the `turnOffCryp-toLogging` method.

```
static void turnOffCryptoLogging() {
  Logger root = Logger.getRootLogger();
  boolean rootIsConfigured = root.getAllAppenders().hasMoreElements();
  if(!rootIsConfigured) {
    Logger.getInstance("com.spookz.cryptolib").setLevel(Level.OFF);
  }
}
```

In this modified version of `turnOffCryptoLogging`, we essentially check if log4j has been already configured by inspecting the root logger to see whether it contains any appenders. If it does, we consider log4j to be already configured and skip the step of turning off logging for the "com.spookz.cryptolib" logger.

The inspection of the root logger is based on the documented properties of the `getAllAppenders` method. The `Logger.getAllAppenders` method returns all the appenders attached to a logger as an `Enumeration`. In case there are no attached appenders, it returns a `NullEnumeration` which contains no elements and whose `hasMoreElements` method always returns `false`, whereas non-empty enumerations are guaranteed to return `true` the first time their `hasMoreElements` method is called.

This technique ensures that the configuration of log4j and turning off logging can be called in any order without mutual interference. However, it assumes that any configuration necessarily adds one or more appenders to the root logger which theoretically may not always be the case. In the unlikely circumstance where log4j is configured without adding at least one appender to the root logger, the appenders-in-root test will not be effective. There is not much that can be done to prevent this, except documenting your working assumptions, namely that at least one appender is assumed to be added to the root logger. In the worst case, the CryptoLib will not produce any logging output even if the deployer's configuration has enabled CryptoLib logging. As a workaround, she can add a `NullAppender`[16] to the root logger. NullAppenders, as the name indicates, merely exist but do not output anything to any device.

The examples for this chapter contain the java files *examples/chapter3/-CryptoLib.java* and *examples/chapter3/CryptoUser.java*. These examples show how a library can coordinate its logging settings with those configured by the end-user. The XML configurations *user1.xml* and *user2.xml* are also included.

Default Initialization

Log4j aims to be a universal logging package for the Java language. This claim to universality prohibits making assumptions about the environment in which log4j executes. Assumptions that seem natural on most platforms can be invalid on others. For example, the JVM on the AS/400 platform does not have a console even if most other Java platforms do. Just as importantly, log4j may lack a mandate to write on the console, which may be reserved for purposes other than logging. Thus, logging to the console may not be always appropriate. Similarly, writing to files from an EJB is forbidden according to the J2EE specification. Given that there is

---

[16] The `NullAppender` class is defined in the `org.apache.log4j.varia` package.

no such thing as a universally available or accepted logging device, log4j does not define a default appender. In essence, log4j must be configured prior to usage. This can be done either programmatically or by invoking a configurator with an appropriate configuration script.

However, some applications have multiple entry points such that it may be cumbersome or even impossible for the user to configure log4j prior to usage. To address this problem, log4j defines a default initialization procedure which configures log4j under well-defined conditions, under the control of the user. Default initialization is performed when log4j classes are loaded into memory, more precisely within the static initializer of the `LogManager` class. The Java language guarantees that the static initializer of a class is called once and only once when loading the class into memory. Since a class must be loaded into memory before usage of the class and since the `LogManager` is directly or indirectly involved in the retrieval of every `Logger` instance, it is guaranteed that default initialization will precede every logging attempt.

Default log4j initialization procedure

The default initialization algorithm is invoked when the `LogManager` class is loaded into memory. This class is guaranteed to be loaded before any logger can be used. The exact initialization algorithm is defined as follows:

- If the **log4j.defaultInitOverride** system property is set to any other value then "false", the default initialization procedure (this procedure) is skipped.

- The value of the **log4j.configuration** system property defines the configuration resource. The value of the **log4j.configuration** system property can be a URL or a file expressed in a system dependent format.

- If the **log4j.configuration** is not defined, then configuration resource *log4j.xml* is searched with the following algorithm:

  Under JDK 1.2 and later, search for the resource using the thread context class loader. If that fails, attempt to locate the resource using the class loader that loaded the log4j library. Failing that, one last attempt is made by calling `ClassLoader.getSystemResource(resource)` method. The result of the search, if successful, is always a URL.

- If the resource *log4j.xml* cannot be located, then search for *log4j.properties* using the above search algorithm.

- If the `log4j.configuration` system property was not defined and no resources *log4j.xml* or *log4j.properties* could be found, then no default initialization can occur.

- Otherwise, if a configuration resource could be found, invoke the `config-ure(URL)` method of the appropriate log4j configurator. If the configuration resource ends with an *.xml* extension, then the `DOMConfigurator` is invoked. Otherwise, the `PropertyConfigurator` is used. The user can optionally specify a custom configurator. The value of the `log4j.configuratorClass` system property is taken as the fully qualified class name of the custom configurator. The custom configurator must implement the `Configurator` interface.

 The file *log4j.xml* is probed for in log4j version 1.2.7 and later. Previous log4j versions only probe for the file *log4j.properties*.

The *MyApp4* application, listed next, does not explicitly configure log4j, relying instead on default initialization.

Example 3-27: Application without explicit configuration (examples/chapter3/MyApp4)

```
package chapter3;
import org.apache.log4j.Logger;

public class MyApp4 {
  final static Logger logger = Logger.getLogger(MyApp4.class);

  public static void main(String[] args) {
    logger.info("Entering application.");
    Foo foo = new Foo();
    foo.doIt();
    logger.info("Exiting application.");
  }
}
```

Running *MyApp4* without prior preparation will result in the following irritating but familiar warning message:

```
log4j:WARN No appenders could be found for logger (chapter3.MyApp4).
log4j:WARN Please initialize the log4j system properly.
```

Default initialization takes place if the **log4j.configuration** system property is set or the file *log4j.xml* or *log4j.properties* is available on the classpath (or to the thread context loader). Assuming *LOG4J_MANUAL/examples/* directory is on the classpath, copy any XML configuration script as *LOG4J_MANUAL*/examples/*log4j.xml*. Similarly, you can copy a properties file as

LOG4J_MANUAL/examples/*log4j.properties*.   Try running *MyApp4* again. You should notice the configuration file being picked up automatically.

It is a common mistake to add the configuration file to the classpath instead of the directory where the configuration file is located. For instance, assuming the file */foo*/*log4j.xml* exists for the purposes of default initialization, adding /foo/*log4j.xml* to the classpath is a mistake, while adding */foo/* is correct.

We can force the default initialization procedure to consider a particular file with the help of the **log4j.configuration** system property. As in,

```
java -Dlog4j.configuration=chapter3/defaultIni.xml chapter3.MyApp4
```

Note that the value of the **log4j.configuration** system property can be a URL. As in,

```
java -Dlog4j.configuration=file:chapter3/defaultIni.xml chapter3.MyApp4
```

Log4j Initialization in Web Containers

The Java Servlet technology is the cornerstone of many server-side applications. For those unfamiliar with Servlets, I highly recommend Jason Hunter's book entitled "Java Servlet Programming" from O'Reilly & Associates.

Although not explicitly stated in the Java Servlet 2.3 and Java Server Pages 1.2 specifications, most web containers will load the classes of a web-application in a separate class loader. Moreover, per section SRV.3.7 of the specification, the container is required to load the servlets and the classes that they may use in the scope of a single class loader. In practice, this means that any utility classes of the web-application will be loaded anew for each web-application. Thus, you may have multiple copies of log4j classes loaded simultaneously. Each such copy will go through the default log4j initialization procedure.

It is important to know that different class loaders may load distinct copies of the same class. These copies of the same class are considered as totally unrelated by the JVM. Class loading is central but rather advanced Java topic. Some familiarity with class loaders is necessary for the pursuit of this discussion. There are several dozen tutorials on the subject of which I recommend the following:

- "The basics of Java class loaders" from *http://www.javaworld.com/javaworld/-jw-10-1996/jw-10-indepth.html*

- "Understanding   `Class.forName()`"   from   *http://www.javageeks.com/-Papers/ClassForName/index.html*

- "EJB 2 and J2EE Packaging, Part II" from *http://www.onjava.com/pub/a/-onjava/ 2001/07/25/ejb.html*

Per section SRV.9.5 of the Java Servlet specification, the web application class loader is required to load any jar files in the *WEB-INF/lib* directory. Moreover, per section SRV.9.7.2, it is recommended classes packaged within the war file be loaded in preference to classes residing in container-wide jar files. In particular, Tomcat 4.x has a class loader hierarchy which makes its own utility classes invisible to web-applications.

Thus, in practice, placing *log4j-VERSION.jar* in the *WEB-INF/lib* directory of your web-application will cause log4j classes to be loaded/unloaded whenever your web-application is loaded/unloaded. Moreover, each copy of the log4j classes will be treated as a separate and unrelated copy by the JVM. It follows that each of your web-applications can live in its own log4j-logging universe.

Default Initialization under Tomcat

The default log4j initialization is particularly useful in web-server environments. In this section, I assume that you have placed *log4j.jar* in the *WEB-INF/lib/* directory of each of your web-applications. Under Tomcat 3.x and 4.x, you should then place the *log4j.xml* or *log4j.properties* under *the WEB-INF/classes* directory of your web-applications. Log4j will find the properties file and initialize itself. This is easy to do and works reasonably well.

As mentioned previously, you can also choose to set the `log4j.configuration` system property before starting Tomcat. For Tomcat 3.x The TOMCAT_OPTS environment variable is used to set command line options. For Tomcat 4.0, set the CATALINA_OPTS environment variable instead of TOMCAT_OPTS.

Relative path configuration file (PropertyConfigurator)

The Unix shell command

```
export TOMCAT_OPTS="-Dlog4j.configuration=foobar.txt"
```

tells log4j to use the file *foobar.txt* as the default configuration file. This file should be place under the *WEB-INF/classes* directory of your web-application. The file will be read using the `PropertyConfigurator`. Each web-application will use a different default configuration file because each file is relative to a web-application.

Relative path configuration file (DOMConfigurator)

The Unix shell command

```
export TOMCAT_OPTS="-Dlog4j.debug -Dlog4j.configuration=foo.xml"
```

tells log4j to output log4j-internal debugging information for the list of searched locations and to use the file *foo.xml* as the default configuration file. This file should be placed under the *WEB-INF/classes/* directory of your web-application. Since the file ends with an *.xml* extension, it will be parsed using the DOMConfigurator. Each web-application will use a different default configuration file because each file is relative to a web-application.

Absolute-path configuration file

The Windows shell command

```
set TOMCAT_OPTS=-Dlog4j.configuration=file:/c:/foobar.lcf
```

tells log4j to use the file *c:\foobar.xml* as the default configuration file. The configuration file is fully specified by the URL *file:/c://foobar.lcf*. Thus, the same configuration file will be used for all web-applications.

Different web-applications will load the log4j classes through their respective class loaders. Thus, each image of the log4j environment will act independently and without any mutual synchronization. This can lead to a dangerous situation. For example, if different web-applications define an appender writing to an absolute-path file, each of those appenders will all write to that file without any mutual synchronization. The results are likely to be less than satisfactory. It is your responsibility to make sure that log4j configurations of different web-applications do not use the same underlying system resource.

More generally, appenders should not share the same system resource. Any appender shipped with log4j is guaranteed to safely handle calls from multiple threads. However, configuring one or more appenders to write to the same file or system resource is unsafe as there is not mutual synchronization between appenders, even if they are running under the same VM.

Initialization servlet

It is also possible to use a special servlet for log4j initialization. Here is an example:

Example 3-28: Initialization servlet (examples/chapter3/Log4jInitServlet.java)

```java
package chapter3;
import org.apache.log4j.PropertyConfigurator;
import javax.servlet.http.HttpServlet;
import javax.servlet.http.HttpServletRequest;
import javax.servlet.http.HttpServletResponse;
import java.io.PrintWriter;
import java.io.IOException;

public class Log4jInitServlet extends HttpServlet {

  public void init() {
    String prefix =  getServletContext().getRealPath("/");
    String file = getInitParameter("log4j-init-file");
    // if the log4j-init-file is not set, then no point in trying
    if(file != null) {
      PropertyConfigurator.configure(prefix+file);
    }
  }

  public void doGet(HttpServletRequest req, HttpServletResponse res) {
  }
}
```

Define the following servlet in the *web.xml* file of your web-application.

```xml
<servlet>
  <servlet-name>log4j-init</servlet-name>
  <servlet-class>chapter3.Log4jInitServlet</servlet-class>

  <init-param>
    <param-name>log4j-init-file</param-name>
    <param-value>WEB-INF/classes/log4j.properties</param-value>
  </init-param>

  <load-on-startup>1</load-on-startup>
</servlet>
```

Writing an initialization servlet is the most flexible way for initializing log4j as there are no constraints on the amount of code you can place in the `init()` method of the servlet.

Log4j Initialization in Application Servers

Log4j is known to work well under most application servers although you should be aware of the classical EJB restrictions. In particular, your class-wide loggers should be final static. As in,

```
public class SomeEJB extends EntityBean {

  final static Logger logger = Logger.gerLogger(SomeEJB.class);
  ...
}
```

You should also avoid using the `FileAppender` because it writes directly to a file. Although writing to files does not seem to cause problems in most application servers, it is explicitly forbidden by the EJB specification. You should consider the `SocketAppender` or `JMSAppender` instead. Similarly, avoid using the `AsyncAppender` because it creates a thread of its own, which is forbidden by the EJB specification.

JBoss

As of version 2.4, JBoss uses log4j for its own logging. Consequently, your own EJBs and web applications will automatically inherit JBoss' log4j configuration.

More often than not you to keep your application's logs separate from the application server's logs. Thus, log4j's adoption by JBoss is a step backward in some sense. Fortunately, there are a number of possible solutions.

The easiest solution is to modify JBoss' log4j configuration file. Assuming all your classes live under "com.wombat" package or in packages under com.wombat, configuring a logger called "com.wombat" and setting its level and additivity will isolate all loggers under it, effectively isolating logging from your code from that of JBoss. For this approach to work properly your code should not make use of the loggers that JBoss uses, such as those under "org.jboss" or the root logger.

Weblogic 6.x

One simple but somewhat inflexible approach for using log4j under Weblogic is to add *log4j.jar* to the system classpath before launching Weblogic server. This is guaranteed to work except that all applications will be sharing the same instance of the log4j classes and consequently share the same log4j configuration. It is also possible to have Weblogic load a separate instance of log4j classes per application. Although not difficult this approach requires some rudimentary understanding of the way Weblogic loads your applications.

Contrary to version 5.x, when Weblogic version 6.x deploys an application, it creates three class loaders: one for EJBs, one for Web applications and one for JSP files. The first, the so called "EJB class loader" is a child of the system class loader. The second, the so called "Web-application" class loader is a child of the EJB class loader. The third class loader, the JSP class loader, is a child of the second. Thus, classes in the web-application can access the classes in your enterprise beans but not vice versa. Please refer to the document Weblogic Class loader Overview at *http://e-docs.bea.com/wls/docs61/programming/* for more details.

As far as I know, contrary to servlet containers which are required to load classes and jar files located under the */WEB-INF/classes* and */WEB-INF/lib* directory, there is no standard location that the EJB container will search in order to load your utility classes. As mentioned earlier, one solution to circumvent this problem is to add log4j to the Java system class path with the aforementioned limitations. Another approach is to include *log4j.jar* within your EJB jar files. This has the distinct disadvantage of bloat.

There is a better and quite elegant approach. Version 1.2 of the Java platform, added support for bundled extensions[17] for jar files. A jar file can specify the relative URLs of extensions and libraries that it requires via the "Class-Path" manifest attribute. Relative URLs ending with '/' are assumed to refer to directories.

For example, adding the line

```
Class-Path: lib/log4j-VERSION.jar lib/
```

to the manifest file of your application's ear file or your EJB jar files will allow log4j classes to be loaded from *lib/log4j-VERSION.jar* relative to the ear or jar file. Placing *log4j.xml* or *log4j.properties* in the *lib/* directory will let log4j find the properties configuration file and auto-initialize.

IBM Websphere

See the Chapter 13 of IBM Redbook "Websphere Version 4 Application Development Handbook" for a discussion on using log4j under WebSphere. Though the Redbook is undoubtedly motivated by the noblest intentions, I strongly discourage you from adopting its initialization wrapper (LogHelper) approach. That particular wrapper solution is highly intrusive and goes against the separation of usage and configuration principle. This approach unfortunately continues to be occasionally suggested by well-meaning users.

---

[17] See: *http://java.sun.com/products/jdk/1.2/docs/guide/extensions/spec.html*

4

APPENDERS

There is so much to tell about the Western country in that day that it is hard to know where to start. One thing sets off a hundred others. The problem is to decide which one to tell first.

—JOHN STEINBECK, *East of Eden*

Log4j delegates the task of writing a logging event to appenders. Appenders must implement the `org.apache.log4j.Appender` interface. The salient methods of this interface are summarized below (getter methods omitted):

```
package org.apache.log4j;

public interface Appender {
   void addFilter(Filter newFilter);
   void clearFilters();
   void close();
   void doAppend(LoggingEvent event);
   boolean requiresLayout();
   void setErrorHandler(ErrorHandler errorHandler);
   void setLayout(Layout layout);
   void setName(String name);
}
```

Most of the methods in the `Appender` interface are made of setter and getter methods. A notable exception is the `doAppend` method taking a `LoggingEvent` instance as its only parameter. This method is perhaps the most important in the log4j framework. It is responsible for outputting the logging event in a suitable format to the appropriate output device. Appenders are named entities. This ensures that they can be referenced by name, a quality confirmed to be especially significant in configuration scripts. All appenders must have an `ErrorHandler` that is responsible for reacting to error conditions. An appender can contain multiple filters, each of which is added by invoking the `addFilter` method. Filters are discussed in detail in a subsequent chapter.

Appenders are ultimately responsible for outputting logging events. However, they may delegate the actual formatting of the event to a `Layout` object. Each layout is associated with one and only one appender, referred to as the containing appender. Some appenders have a built-in or fixed event format, such that they do not require a layout. For example, the `SocketAppender` and `JMSAppender` simply serialize `LoggingEvent` objects before transmitting them over the wire. Developers of custom appenders should make sure that if their custom appender does not require a layout, then the `requiresLayout` method of their appender returns `false` as a value. Failure to do so will cause log4j configurators (e.g. `DOMConfigurator`) to complain about missing layout information even if the custom appender does not need a layout.

AppenderSkeleton

The `AppenderSkeleton` class is an abstract class implementing the `Appender` interface. It provides basic functionality shared by all appenders, such as methods for getting or setting their name, their threshold, their layout, their filters and their error handler. It is the super-class of all appenders shipped with log4j. Although an abstract class, `AppenderSkeleton` actually implements the `doAppend()` method in the `Append` interface. Perhaps the clearest way to discuss `AppenderSkeleton` class is by presenting actual source code.

```
public synchronized void doAppend(LoggingEvent event) {
   if(closed) {
     LogLog.error("Attempted to append to closed appender ["
                  +name+"].");
     return;
   }
   if(!isAsSevereAsThreshold(event.level)) {
     return;
   }
   Filter f = this.headFilter;
   FILTER_LOOP:
   while(f != null) {
     switch(f.decide(event)) {
     case Filter.DENY: return;
     case Filter.ACCEPT: break FILTER_LOOP;
     case Filter.NEUTRAL: f = f.next;
     }
   }
   this.append(event);
}
```

This implementation of the `doAppend` method is synchronized. It follows that logging to the same appender from different threads is safe. While a thread, say *T*, is executing the doAppend method, subsequent calls by other threads are queued until *T* leaves the doAppend method, ensuring *T*'s exclusive access to the appender.

The first statement in the doAppend method checks whether the "closed" field is true. If it is, doAppend will output a warning message on the console and return. In other words, once closed, it is impossible to write to a closed appender. Sub-classes of AppenderSkeleton are required to set the boolean variable "closed" to true when their close() method is invoked. The next if statement checks whether the log event is below the threshold of the appender. If so, the method returns without taking any further action. Otherwise, the method loops through the filters attached to the appender. Depending on the decision made by the filters in the filter chain, events can be denied or alternatively accepted. In the absence of a decision by the filter chain, events are accepted by default.

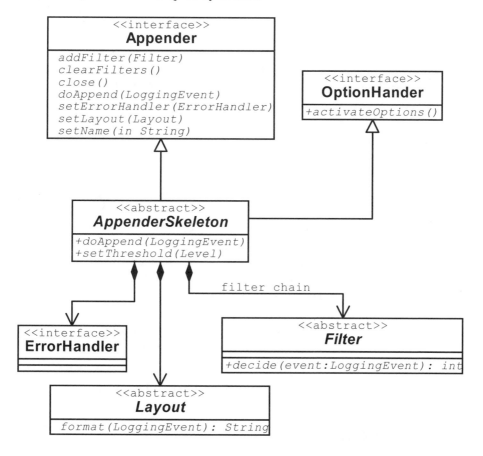

Figure 4-1: Simplified UML class diagram of AppenderSkeleton class

The simplified UML class diagram in *Figure 4-1* illustrates `AppenderSkeleton`'s relation to other classes, omitting all class attributes and getter methods. Appenders delegate the processing of error conditions to an `ErrorHandler` object. By default, the `AppenderSkeleton` sets the error handler to a `OnceOnlyErrorHandler` which prints a single warning message on the console when the first error occurs, ignoring any subsequent errors.

Note that `AppenderSkeleton` also implements the `OptionHandler` interface. This interface contains a single method, namely `activateOptions()`. After setting all the options of an appender, a configurator calls this method to signal the appender to bind or activate its options. Indeed, depending on the appender, certain options cannot be activated because of interferences with other options. For example, since file creation depends on truncation mode, `FileAppender` cannot act on the value of its **File** option until the value of the **Append** option is also known for certain.

The term *option* or *property* is reserved for named attributes that are dynamically inferred using JavaBeans introspection. Please also refer to **Q 10.10** of the FAQ on page 190. `AppenderSkeleton` offers just a single albeit important option.

Option Name	Type	Description
Threshold	`Level`	If the **Threshold** option is set, the events below the threshold level are ignored. In configuration scripts level values can be one of the case insensitive strings "ALL", "DEBUG", "INFO", WARN", "ERROR", FATAL, "OFF" or a custom level value. A custom level value can be specified in the form "level#classname". The standard level strings are case insensitive while the classname part of a custom level is case sensitive.
		By default, the **Threshold** option is set to `null` meaning that all events pass the appender threshold unhindered.

All sub-classes of `AppenderSkeleton` inherit the **Threshold** option.

WriterAppender

`WriterAppender` appends events to a `java.io.Writer`. This class provides basic services that other appenders build upon. Users do not usually instantiate `WriterAppender` objects directly. Since `java.io.Writer` type cannot be mapped to a string, there is no way to specify the target `Writer` object in a configuration script. Simply put, you cannot configure a `WriterAppender` from a script. However, this does not mean that `WriterAppender` lacks configurable options. These options are described next.

Option Name	Type	Description
Encoding	`String`	The encoding specifies the method of conversion between 16-bit Unicode characters into raw 8-bit bytes. This appender will use the local platform's default encoding unless you specify otherwise using the **Encoding** option. According to the `java.lang` package documentation, acceptable values are dependent on the VM implementation although all implementations are required to support at least the following encodings: "US-ASCII", "ISO-8859-1", "UTF-8", "UTF-16BE", "UTF-16LE" and "UTF-16". By default, the **Encoding** option is `null` such that the platform's default encoding is used.
ImmediateFlush	`boolean`	If set to `true`, each write of a `LoggingEvent` is followed by a flush operation on the underlying `Writer` object. Conversely, if the option is set to `false`, each write will not be followed by a flush. In general, skipping the flush operation improves logging throughput by roughly 15%. The downside is that if the application exits abruptly, the unwritten characters buffered inside `Writer` might be lost. This can be particularly troublesome as those unwritten characters may contain crucial information needed in identifying the reasons behind a crash.[18] By default, the **ImmediateFlush** option is set to `true`.
Threshold	`Level`	See options for `AppenderSkeleton`.

---

[18] I doubt that a blackbox on an airplane uses buffered I/O to persist flight data.

In general, if you disable immediate flushing, then make sure to flush any output streams when your application exits. Otherwise, log messages will be lost as illustrated by the next example.

Example 4-1: Exiting an application without flushing *(examples/chapter4/ExitWoes1.java)*

```
package chapter4;
import org.apache.log4j.*;
import java.io.*;

/**
 * A simple application that illustrates loss of logging data when
 * exiting an application without flushing i/o buffers.
 * */
public class ExitWoes1 {

  public static void main(String argv[]) throws Exception {

    WriterAppender writerAppender = new WriterAppender();
    writerAppender.setLayout(new SimpleLayout());
    OutputStream os = new FileOutputStream("exitWoes1.log");
    writerAppender.setWriter(new OutputStreamWriter(os));
    writerAppender.setImmediateFlush(false);
    writerAppender.activateOptions();

    Logger logger = Logger.getLogger(ExitWoes1.class);
    logger.addAppender(writerAppender);

    logger.debug("Hello world.");
  }
}
```

This example creates a `WriterAppender` that uses an `OutputStreamWriter` wrapping a `FileOutputStream` as its underlying `Writer` object, with immediate flushing disabled. It then attaches this appender to a logger and proceeds to log a single debug message. According to `OutputStreamWriter` javadocs, each invocation of a `write()` method causes the encoding converter to be invoked on the given character(s). The resulting bytes are accumulated in a buffer before being written to the underlying output stream. As astonishing as this may seem, running *ExitWoes1* will not produce any output in the file *exitWoes1.log* because the Java VM does not flush output streams when it exits. Calling the `shutdown()` method of a `LoggerRepository` ensures that all appenders in the hierarchy are closed and their buffers are flushed. For most applications this is as simple as including the following statement before exiting the application.

```
LogManager.getLoggerRepository().shutdown();
```

See the file `examples/chapter4/ExitWoes2.java` for a complete example.

The `WriterAppender` is the super class of four other appenders, namely `ConsoleAppender`, `FileAppender` which in turn is the super class of `RollingFileAppender` and also `DailyRollingFileAppender`. Figure 4-2 illustrates the class diagram for `WriterAppender` and its subclasses.

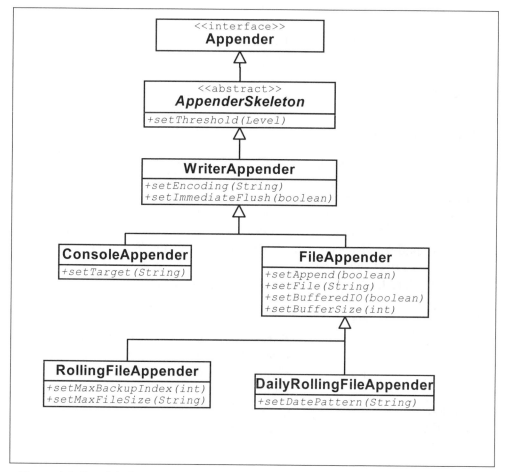

Figure 4-2: Simplified class diagram for WriterAppender and its derived classes.

ConsoleAppender

The `ConsoleAppender`, as the name indicates, appends on the console, or more precisely on `System.out` or `System.err`, the former being the default target. `ConsoleAppender` formats events with a layout specified by the user. Both `System.out` and `System.err` are `java.io.PrintStream` objects. Consequently, they are wrapped inside an `OutputStreamWriter` which buffers I/O operations but not character conversions.

Option Name	Type	Description
Encoding	String	See `WriterAppender` options.
ImmediateFlush	boolean	There is not much sense in buffered console I/O, so leaving this option at its default (true) is usually appropriate.
Target	String	One of the `String` values "System.out" or "System.err". The default target is `System.out`.
Threshold	Level	See `AppenderSkeleton` options.

FileAppender

The `FileAppender`, a subclass of `WriterAppender`, appends log events into a file. The file to write to is specified by the **File** option. If the file already exists, it is either appended to, or truncated depending on the value of the **Append** option. It uses a `FileOutputStream` which is wrapped by an `OutputStreamWriter`. Note that `OutputStreamWriter` buffers I/O operations but not character conversions. To optimize character conversions one can set the **BufferedIO** option to `true` which effectively wraps the `OutputStreamWriter` with a `BufferedWriter`. Options for `FileAppender` are summarized below.

Option Name	Type	Description
Append	Boolean	If true, events are appended at the end of an existing file. Otherwise, if **Append** is `false`, any existing file is truncated. The **Append** option is set to `true` by default.
Encoding	String	See `WriterAppender` options.
BufferedIO	Boolean	The **BufferedIO** option is set to `false` by default. If set to `true`, the underlying `OutputStreamWriter` is wrapped by a `BufferedWriter` object. Setting **BufferedIO** to `true` automatically sets the **ImmediateFlush** option to `false`. The name **BufferedIO** is slightly misleading because buffered IO is already supported by `OutputStreamWriter`. Setting **BufferedIO** to `true` has the effect of buffering I/O as well as character to raw byte conversions, saving a few CPU cycles in the process.

BufferSize	`int`	Size of `BufferedWriter` buffer. The default value is 8192.
File	`String`	The name of the file to write to. If the file does not exist, it is created.
		On the MS Windows platform users frequently forget to escape back slashes. For example, the value "c:\temp\test.log" is not likely to be interpreted properly as '\t' is an escape sequence interpreted as a single tab character (\u0009). Correct values can be specified as `c:/temp/test.log` or alternatively as `c:\\temp\\test.log`.
		The File option has no default value.
ImmediateFlush	`Boolean`	See `WriterAppender` options.
Threshold	`Level`	See `AppenderSkeleton` options.

By default, `FileAppender` performs a flush operation for each event, ensuring that events are immediately written to disk. Setting the ImmediateFlush option to `false` can drastically reduce I/O activity by letting `OutputStreamWriter` buffer bytes before writing them on disk. For short messages, I have observed 2 or 3 fold increases in logging throughput, i.e. the number of logs output per unit of time. For longer messages, the throughput gains are somewhat less dramatic, and range between 1.4 and 2 fold. Enabling the BufferedIO option, that is buffering character to byte conversions, increases performance by an additional 10% to 40% compared to only disk I/O buffering (ImmediateFlush=false). Performance varies somewhat depending on the host machine as well as JDK version. Throughput measurements are based on the *chapter4.IO* application. Please refer to the file *examples/chapter4/IO.java* for actual source code.

RollingFileAppender

`RollingFileAppender` extends `FileAppender` by limiting the size of log files to a user specified length. Logging output is written to the file specified by the File option. When the log file reaches the specified size, it is rolled over: it is renamed by appending ".1" to the file name. If a ".1" file exists, it is first renamed to ".2" and so on. For example, if the File option is set to *wombat.log*, then *wombat.log* will be renamed as *wombat.log.1*. Any existing *wombat.log.1* file is renamed as *wombat.log.2*, any previously existing *wombat.log.2* file is renamed to *wombat.log.3* and so on, until MaxBackupIndex. For instance, assuming MaxBackupIndex is set to 4, *wombat.log.4* is simply deleted without further cascading.

Thus, in addition to the `FileAppender` options, `RollingFileAppender` has two additional options, MaxFileSize and MaxBackupIndex, as summarized below.

Option Name	Type	Description
Append	`Boolean`	See `FileAppender` options.
Encoding	`String`	See `WriterAppender` options.
BufferedIO	`Boolean`	See `FileAppender` options.
BufferSize	`int`	See `FileAppender` options.
File	`String`	See `FileAppender` options.
ImmediateFlush	`Boolean`	See `WriterAppender` options.
MaxBackupIndex	`int`	The MaxBackupIndex option determines the number of log files to preserve. This option takes a positive integer value. If set to zero, no roll over occurs and the log file is simply truncated when it reaches MaxFileSize. The MaxBackupIndex option is set to 1 by default. For efficiency reasons, the value of the MaxBackupIndex option should not surpass 10. Consider increasing MaxFileSize instead of MaxBackupIndex.
MaxFileSize	`String`	The MaxFileSize option takes a `String` value representing a long integer in the range $0 - 2^{63}$. You can also specify the value with the suffixes "KB", "MB" or "GB" so that the integer is interpreted as being expressed respectively in kilobytes, megabytes or gigabytes. For example, the value "10KB" will be interpreted as 10240.
		Rollover occurs when the log file reaches MaxFileSize. Note that since the last log event is written entirely before a roll over is triggered, actual files are usually a tad larger than the exact value of MaxFileSize.
		The default value of this option is 10MB.
Threshold	`Level`	See `AppenderSkeleton` options.

A simple example, *chapter4.Rolling*, is included under the *examples/chapter4/* directory. It configures log4j by reading a configuration file in either properties or XML format, and proceeds to loop until the number of log events specified by the user are generated. The user should consult the configuration files *rolling.properties* and *rolling.xml* included in the same directory for short examples of `RollingFileAppender` configuration.

Using `RollingFileAppender` system administrators can control the size of log files. Understandably, volume is not a common criterion for organizing log files; most system administrators prefer to structure log files by date.

DailyRollingFileAppender

`DailyRollingFileAppender` extends `FileAppender` in order to roll files at user chosen time intervals. The rolling schedule is specified by the **DatePattern** option. This pattern should follow the `java.text.SimpleDateFormat` conventions. In particular, you must escape literal text within a pair of single quotes. The formatted version of the date pattern is used as the suffix for the rolled file name. For example, if the **File** option is set to */foo/bar.log* and the **DatePattern** set to '.'yyyy-MM-dd, then at midnight 2002-06-19, the file */foo/bar.log* will be copied to /foo/bar.log.2002-06-19 and logging during 2001-06-20 will continue in */foo/bar.log* until it is in turn rolled over the next day.

One can specify monthly, weekly, half-daily, daily, hourly, or even minutely roll-over schedules. The table below lists various **DatePattern** values as well as the resulting rollover intervals and file names.

DatePattern	Result
`.yyyy-MM`	Rollover at the beginning of each month.
	Example: On April 1st 2002, 00:00 AM, the file `/foo/bar.log` will be copied to */foo/bar.log.2002-03*. Logging for the month of April will be output to `/foo/bar.log` until it rolls over at the beginning of May.
`.yyyy-ww`	Rollover at the first day of each week. The first day of the week depends on the locale.
	Example: Assuming the first day of the week is Sunday, at the end of the 23rd week of 2002 that is on Sunday morning 00:00 AM, June 9th 2002, the file */foo/bar.log* will be copied to */foo/bar.log.2002-23*. Logging for the 24th week of 2002 will be output to `/foo/bar.log` until it is rolled over at the beginning of the next week.
`.yyyy-MM-dd`	Rollover at midnight each day.
	Example: At midnight March 7th, 2002, */foo/bar.log* will be copied to */foo/bar.log.2002-03-07*. Logging for the 8th day of March will be output to `/foo/bar.log` until it is rolled over at the start of the next day.
`.yyyy-MM-dd-a`	Rollover at midnight and midday of each day.
	Example: At noon May 11th 2002, */foo/bar.log* will be

	copied to */foo/bar.log.2002-05-11-AM*. Logging for the afternoon of the 11th will be output to `/foo/bar.log` until it is rolled over at midnight.
`.yyyy-MM-dd-HH`	Rollover at the top of every hour. Example: At approximately 11:00,000, on July 4th, 2002, the file */foo/bar.log* will be copied to */foo/bar.log.2002-06-04-10*. Logging for the 11th hour of the 4th of July will be output to */foo/bar.log* until it is rolled over at the beginning of the next hour.
`.yyyy-MM-dd-HH-mm`	Rollover at the beginning of every minute. Example: At approximately 11:23.000 o'clock on March 9th 2002, the file */foo/bar.log* will be copied to */foo/bar.log.2002-03-09-11-22*. Logging during 11:23, that is one minute, will be output to */foo/bar.log* until it is rolled over at start of the next minute.

Thus, the **DatePattern** serves two purposes. First, by studying the pattern log4j computes the requested rollover periodicity. Second, it uses the pattern as the suffix for rolled files. It is entirely possible for two different date patterns to specify the same periodicity. The date patterns ".yyyy-MM" and "-yyyy@MM" both specify monthly rollover periodicity, although the rolled files will carry different suffixes.

Any characters in the pattern outside the ranges ['a'..'z'] and ['A'..'Z'] will be treated as quoted text. For instance, characters like '.', ' ', '#' and '@' will appear in the resulting time text even when they are not enclosed within single quotes. Nevertheless, I would recommend against using the colon ":" character anywhere within the **DatePattern** option. The text before the colon is interpreted as the protocol specification of a URL, which is most probably not what you intend. The slash "/" character, a common date field separator, must also be avoided. It is taken as a file separator causing the rollover operation to fail because the target file cannot be created. Although less common, the backslash character "\" is equally troublesome.

The `DailyRollingFileAppender` adds just one option, namely the **DatePattern** option, to the list of options supported by `FileAppender`. This is summarized in the table below.

Option Name	Type	Description
Append	Boolean	See `FileAppender` options.
DatePattern	String	The **DatePattern** option controls the rollover frequency as the as the suffix of the rolled over log files. The pattern should follow the conventions of the `java.text.SimpleDateFormat` class. By default the **DatePattern** option is set to .yyyy-MM-dd (daily rollover).
Encoding	String	See `WriterAppender` options.
BufferedIO	Boolean	See `FileAppender` options.
BufferSize	int	See `FileAppender` options.
File	String	See `FileAppender` options.
ImmediateFlush	Boolean	See `WriterAppender` options.
Threshold	Level	See `AppenderSkeleton` options.

For various efficiency reasons, rollovers are not time-driven but depend on the arrival of logging events. For example, on 8th of March 2002, assuming the **DatePattern** is set to .yyyy-MM-dd (daily rollover), the arrival of the first event after midnight will trigger rollover. If there are no logging events during, say 23 minutes and 47 seconds after midnight, then rollover will occur at 00:23'47 AM on March 9th and not at 0:00 AM. Thus, depending on the arrival rate of events, rollovers might be triggered with some latency. However, regardless of the delay, the rollover algorithm is known to be correct, in the sense that all logging events generated during a certain period will be output in the correct file delimiting that period.

A simple example, *chapter4.Periodic*, is included under the *examples/chapter4/* directory. It configures log4j by reading a configuration file in either properties or XML format, and then enters an infinite loop generating one log event every 120 seconds. Included in the same directory, the user shall find sample configuration files *periodicX.properties* and *periodicX.xml*, with X representing integer values in the range 1 to 3.

SocketAppender

The appenders covered this far were only able to log to local resources. In contrast, the `SocketAppender` is designed to log to a remote entity by transmitting serialized `LoggingEvent` objects over the wire. Remote logging is non-intrusive as far as the logging event is concerned. On the receiving end after de-serialization, the event can be logged as if it were generated locally. Multiple `SocketAppender` instances running of different machines can direct their logging output to a central log server. `SocketAppender` does not admit an associated layout because it sends serialized events to a remote server. `SocketAppender` operates above the Transmission Control Protocol (TCP) layer which provides a reliable, sequenced, flow-controlled end-to-end octet stream. Consequently, if the remote server is reachable, then log events will eventually arrive there. Otherwise, if the remote server is down or unreachable, the logging events will simply be dropped. If and when the server comes back up, then event transmission will be resumed transparently. This transparent reconnection is performed by a connector thread which periodically attempts to connect to the server.

Logging events are automatically buffered by the native TCP implementation. This means that if the link to server is slow but still faster than the rate of event production by the client, the client will not be affected by the slow network connection. However, if the network connection is slower then the rate of event production, then the client can only progress at the network rate. In particular, in the extreme case where the network link to the server is down, the client will be eventually blocked. Alternatively, if the network link is up, but the server is down, the client will not be blocked although the log events will be lost due to server unavailability.

Even if a `SocketAppender` is no longer attached to any logger, it will not be garbage collected in the presence of a connector thread. A connector thread exists only if the connection to the server is down. To avoid this garbage collection problem, you should close the `SocketAppender` explicitly. Long lived applications which create/destroy many `SocketAppender` instances should be aware of this garbage collection problem. Most other applications can safely ignore it. If the JVM hosting the `SocketAppender` exits before the `SocketAppender` is closed, either explicitly or subsequent to garbage collection, then there might be untransmitted data in the pipe which may be lost. This is a common problem on Windows based systems. To avoid lost data, it is usually sufficient to `close()` the `SocketAppender` either explicitly or by calling the `LogManager.shutdown()` method before exiting the application.

The remote server is identified by the **RemoteHost** and **Port** options. `SocketAppender` options are listed in the following table.

Option Name	Type	Description
LocationInfo	`boolean`	The **LocationInfo** option takes a boolean value. If true, the information sent to the remote host will include location information. By default no location information is sent to the server.
Port	`int`	The port number of the remote server.

ReconnectionDelay	`int`	The ReconnectionDelay option takes a positive integer representing the number of milliseconds to wait between each failed connection attempt to the server. The default value of this option is 30'000 which corresponds to 30 seconds. Setting this option to zero turns off reconnection capability. Note that in case of successful connection to the server, there will be no connector thread present.
RemoteHost	`String`	The host name of the server.
Threshold	`Level`	See `AppenderSkeleton` options.

The standard log4j distribution includes a simple log server application named `org.apache.log4j.net.SimpleSocketServer` that can service multiple `SocketAppender` clients. It waits for logging events from `SocketAppender` clients. After reception by `SimpleSocketServer`, the events are logged according to local server policy. The `SimpleSocketServer` application takes two parameters: *port* and *configFile*; where *port* is the port to listen on and *configFile* is configuration script in properties or XML format.

Assuming you are in the *LOG4J_MANUAL/examples* directory, start `Simple-SocketServer` with the following command:

```
java org.apache.log4j.net.SimpleSocketServer 6000 \
    chapter4/server1.xml
```

where 6000 is the port number to listen on and *server1.xml* is a configuration script that adds a `ConsoleAppender` and a `RollingFileAppender` to the root logger. After you have started `SimpleSocketServer`, you can send it log events from multiple clients using `SocketAppender`. The examples associated with this manual include two such clients: `chapter4.SocketClient1` and `chapter4.SocketClient2`. Both clients wait for the user to type a line of text on the console. The text is encapsulated in a logging event of level debug and then sent to the remote server. The two clients differ in the configuration of the `SocketAppender`. `SocketClient1` configures the appender programmatically while `SocketClient2` requires a configuration file.

Assuming `SimpleSocketServer` is running on the local host, you connect to it with the following command:

```
java -Dlog4j.debug chapter4.SocketClient1 localhost 6000
```

Each line that you type should appear on the console of the `SimpleSocket-Server` launched in the previous step. If you stop and restart the `SimpleSocket-Server` the client will transparently reconnect to the new server instance, although the events generated while disconnected will be simply and irrevocably lost.

Unlike `SocketClient1`, the sample application `SocketClient2` does not configure log4j by itself. It requires a configuration file, either in properties or XML format. The configuration file *client1.xml* shown below creates a `SocketAppender` and attaches it to the root logger.

Example 4-2: SocketAppender configuration *(examples/chapter4/client1.xml)*

```
<?xml version="1.0" encoding="UTF-8"?>
<!DOCTYPE log4j:configuration SYSTEM "log4j.dtd">

<log4j:configuration debug="true"
                    xmlns:log4j='http://jakarta.apache.org/log4j/'>

  <appender name="SOCKET"
          class="org.apache.log4j.net.SocketAppender">
    <param name="RemoteHost" value="${host}"/>
    <param name="Port" value="${port}"/>
  </appender>

  <root>
    <level value ="debug"/>
    <appender-ref ref="SOCKET" />
  </root>
</log4j:configuration>
```

Note that in the above configuration scripts the values for the **RemoteHost** and **Port** options are not given directly but as substituted variable keys. The values for the variables can be specified as system properties:

```
java -Dhost=localhost -Dport=6000 chapter4.SocketClient2 \
  chapter4/client1.xml
```

This command should give similar results to the previous `SocketClient1` example.

Allow me to repeat for emphasis that serialization of logging events is *not* intrusive. A de-serialized event carries the same information as any other logging event. It can be manipulated as if it were generated locally; except that serialized logging events *by default* do not include location information. Here is an example to illustrate the point. First, start `SimpleSocketServer` with the following command:

```
java org.apache.log4j.net.SimpleSocketServer 6000 \
  chapter4/server2.xml
```

The configuration file *server2.xml* creates a `ConsoleAppender` whose layout outputs the callers file name and line number along with other information. If you run `SocketClient2` with the configuration file *client1.xml* as previously, you will notice that the output on the server side will contain two question marks between parentheses instead of the file name and the line number of the caller:

```
2002-06-19 22:36:48,181 DEBUG [main] (?:?) chapter4.SocketClient2 - Hi
```

The outcome can be easily changed by instructing the `SocketAppender` to include location information by setting the **LocationInfo** option to true. Refer to the configuration file *examples/chapter4/client2.xml* for an example.

As deserialized events can be handled in the same way as locally generated events, they even can be sent to a second server for further treatment. As an exercise, you may wish to setup two servers where the first server tunnels the events it receives from its clients to a second server.

JMSAppender

The `JMSAppender` conceptually accomplishes the same task as the `SocketAppender` but as the name suggests it is based on the JMS API instead of TCP sockets. JMS™ or the Java

> The following discussion of `JMSAppender` applies to log4j version 1.2.6 or later.

Message Service API provides an abstraction for Message-Oriented Middleware (MOM) products. One of the key architectural concepts in JMS is the decoupling of message producers and message consumers. Senders do not have to wait for receivers to handle messages and conversely the receiver consumes messages as they become available; messages are said to be delivered asynchronously. Just as importantly, consumers as well as producers can be added or removed at will to a JMS channel. The set of the message producers and message consumers can vary independently and transparently over time, with both sets oblivious to each other.

The JMS specification provides for two types of messaging models, publish-and-subscribe and point-to-point queuing. At the time of this writing, log4j only supports the publish-and-subscribe model[19]. The `JMSAppender` publishes serialized

---

[19] It would be very easy to add support for the queuing model as well. The implementation of a `JMSQueueAppender` is left as an exercise to the reader.

events to a topic specified by the user. One or more `JMSSink` applications can con-
sume these serialized events, as illustrated in Figure 4-3 below.

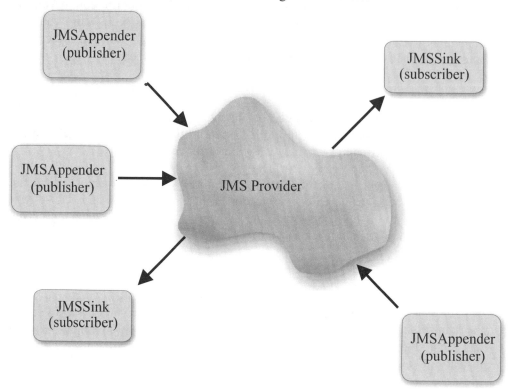

Figure 4-3: JMSAppender/JMSSink architecture

The consumer of `JMSAppender` generated events need not be only `JMSSink` applications. Any application or `MessageDrivenBean` capable of subscribing to the
appropriate topic and consuming serialized logging event messages would be suitable. However, the only consumer that ships with the log4j distribution is the
`org.apache.log4j.net.JMSSink` application. Additional consumers could be
quickly built based on the `JMSSink` model.

The `doAppend` method in `AppenderSkeleton` delegates the task of outputting
data to the `append()` method of its derived classes. The `append()` method of
`JMSAppender` is listed below.

```
public void append(LoggingEvent event) {
  if(!checkEntryConditions()) {
    return;
  }
  try {
    ObjectMessage msg = topicSession.createObjectMessage();
    if(locationInfo) {
      event.getLocationInformation();
    }
    msg.setObject(event);
    topicPublisher.publish(msg);
  } catch(Exception e) {
    errorHandler.error("Could not publish message in JMSAppender ["
                    +name+"].", e, ErrorCode.GENERIC_FAILURE);
  }
}
```

The checkEntryConditions() method checks whether prerequisite conditions for the proper functioning of the JMSAppender, in particular the availability of a valid and open TopicConnection and a TopicSession, are fulfilled. If that is not the case, the append method returns without performing any work. If the prerequisite conditions are fulfilled, then the method proceeds to publish the logging event. This is done by obtaining a javax.jms.ObjectMessage from the TopicSession and then setting its payload to the logging event received as the input parameter. Once the payload of the message is set, it is published. The fact that LoggingEvent is serializable has its importance, as only Serializable objects can be transported within an ObjectMessage.

In summary, the JMSAppender broadcasts messages consisting of a serialized LoggingEvent payload over a user-specified JMS topic. These events can be processed by a JMSSink or a similar consumer. According to JMS specification, the provider will asynchronously call the onMessage() of duly registered and subscribed javax.jms.MessageListener objects. The onMessage() method in JMSSink is implemented as follows:

```
public void onMessage(javax.jms.Message message) {
   Logger remoteLogger;

   if(message instanceof  ObjectMessage) {
      ObjectMessage objMessage = (ObjectMessage) message;
      LoggingEvent event =
                      (LoggingEvent) objMessage.getObject();
      remoteLogger = Logger.getLogger(event.getLoggerName());
         remoteLogger.callAppenders(event);
   } else {
         logger.warn("Received message is of type"
                     + message.getJMSType()
                     + ", was expecting ObjectMessage.");

   }
 }
}
```

The onMessage() method begins by retrieving the logging event's payload. It
then obtains a Logger with the same name as the logger name of the incoming
event. The event is then logged through this logger as if it were generated locally,
by calling its callAppenders() method. The SocketNode class used by Sim-
pleSocketServer handles incoming logging events essentially in the same way.

JMS topics and topic connection factories are administered objects that are obtained using the JNDI API. This in turn implies the necessity of retrieving a JNDI
Context. There are two common methods for obtaining a JNDI Context. If a file
resource named *jndi.properties* is available to the JNDI API, it will use the information found therein to retrieve an initial JNDI context. To obtain an initial context, one simply calls:

```
InitialContext jndiContext = new InitialContext();
```

Calling the no-argument InitialContext() constructor will also work from
within Enterprise Java Beans (EJBs). Indeed, it is part of the EJB contract for application servers to provide each enterprise bean an environment naming context
(ENC).

In the second approach, several predetermined properties are specified. These
properties are passed to the InitialContext constructor to connect to the naming service provider. For example, to connect to the JBoss naming service one
would write:

```
Properties env = new Properties( );
env.put(Context.INITIAL_CONTEXT_FACTORY,
        "org.jnp.interfaces.NamingContextFactory");
env.put(Context.PROVIDER_URL, "jnp://hostname:1099");
```

```
env.put(Context.URL_PKG_PREFIXES,
        "org.jboss.naming:org.jnp.interfaces");
InitialContext jndiContext = new InitialContext(env);
```

where *hostname* is the host where the JBoss application server is running.

To connect to the naming service of Weblogic application server one would write:

```
Properties env = new Properties( );
env.put(Context.INITIAL_CONTEXT_FACTORY,
        "weblogic.jndi.WLInitialContextFactory");
env.put(Context.PROVIDER_URL, "t3://hostname:7001");
InitialContext jndiContext = new InitialContext(env);
```

Other JNDI providers will obviously require different values. As mentioned previously, the initial JNDI context can be obtained by calling the no-argument `InitialContext()` constructor from within EJBs. Only clients running in a separate JVM need to be concerned about the *jndi.properties* file or setting the different properties before calling `InitialContext` constructor taking a `Properties` (i.e. `Hashtable`) parameter.

The remote server is identified by the **RemoteHost** and **Port** options. `SocketAppender` options are listed in the following table.

Option Name	Type	Description
LocationInfo	boolean	The **LocationInfo** option takes a boolean value. If true, the information published on the JMS topic will include location information. By default no location information included in the published message.
InitialContextFactoryName	String	The class name of the initial JNDI context factory. There is no need to set this option if you have a properly configured *jndi.properties* file or if `JMSAppender` is running within an application server. If you set this option, you should also set the **ProviderURL** option.

ProviderURL	String	This option specifies configuration information for the JNDI service provider. The value of the property should contain a URL string (e.g. "ldap://somehost:389").
		The ProviderURL option is taken into account only if the InitialContextFactoryName option is specified. It is ignored otherwise.
URLPkgPrefixes	String	This option contains the list of package prefixes to use when loading in URL context factories. The value of the property should be a colon-separated list of package prefixes for the class name of the URL context factory class.
		For JBoss the value of this option should be: org.jboss.naming:org.jnp.interfaces This option is not needed under Weblogic.
		This option is taken into account only if the InitialContextFactoryName option is specified. It is ignored otherwise.
SecurityPrincipal-Name	String	The security principal name to use when accessing the JNDI namespace. This option is usually not required.
		This option is taken into account only if the InitialContextFactoryName option is specified. It is ignored otherwise.
SecurityCreden-tials	String	The security credentials to use when accessing the JNDI namespace. This option is usually not required.
		This option is taken into account only if both the InitialContextFactoryName and SecurityPrincipalName options are specified. It is ignored otherwise.
TopicFactoryBind-ingName	String	The name of the topic factory. There is no default value for this mandatory option.
TopicBindingName	String	The name of the topic to use. There is no default value for this mandatory option.
UserName	String	The username to use when creating a topic connection.

Password	String	The password to use when creating a topic connection.
Threshold	Level	See AppenderSkeleton options.

Setting up JMSAppender with Weblogic (tested with version 6.1)

First, you must ensure that a JMS connection factory and a JMS topic are properly configured. Let us assume that their JNDI names are "testConnectionFactory" and "testTopic" respectively. This can be accomplished through the Weblogic server administrative console.

Once that is done, start the JMSSink in a command window. The examples accompanying this manual include a Weblogic specific *jndi.properties* file in the *examples/resources/weblogic/* directory. Its contents are reproduced below.

```
java.naming.factory.initial=weblogic.jndi.WLInitialContextFactory
# Change "localhost" to the name of the host running the Weblogic
# server.
java.naming.provider.url=t3://localhost:7001
```

Your next step should be to add the *examples/resources/weblogic/* directory to your CLASSPATH. Also make sure that *weblogic.jar* is in your CLASSPATH.

Changing the directory to *LOG4J_MANUAL/examples/* and assuming a user named "guest" with password "guest" is configured on the Weblogic server, the following command will launch a JMSSink instance.

```
java org.apache.log4j.net.JMSSink testConnectionFactory testTopic \
    guest guest chapter4/jmssink.xml
```

The last argument, that is *chapter4/jmssink.xml*, specifies the path of a configuration file. JMSSink will log the incoming logging events according to the logging policy set by *chapter4/jmssink.xml*. This configuration file simply adds a ConsoleAppender to the root logger, causing each incoming logging event received from various clients to be output on the console. The main point to note about this file is that it is a configuration file like any other. It contains no JMS specific information.

Once an event consumer is available, a producer of logging events can be launched. The JMSAppender produces logging events. We will attach a JMSAppender to a simple application called chapter4.LogStdin included with this manual. This application reads the input typed on the console line by line. Each line is then logged at the debug level. The LogStdin admits one parameter, the path to a configuration file. The configuration file *weblogic.xml* listed below creates a `JMSAppender` with the appropriate options. This appender is then attached to the root logger.

Example 4-3: JMSAppender configuration   for Weblogic *(examples/chapter4/weblogic.xml)*

```xml
<?xml version="1.0" encoding="UTF-8" ?>
<!DOCTYPE log4j:configuration SYSTEM "log4j.dtd">

<log4j:configuration debug="true"
                     xmlns:log4j='http://jakarta.apache.org/log4j/'>

  <appender name="JMS" class="org.apache.log4j.net.JMSAppender">

    <param name="InitialContextFactoryName"
           value="weblogic.jndi.WLInitialContextFactory"/>
    <param name="ProviderURL" value="t3://localhost:7001"/>
    <param name="TopicConnectionFactoryBindingName"
           value="testConnectionFactory"/>
    <param name="TopicBindingName" value="testTopic"/>
    <param name="UserName" value="guest"/>
    <param name="Password" value="guest"/>
    <param name="LocationInfo" value="true"/>
  </appender>

  <root>
    <level value ="debug"/>
    <appender-ref ref="JMS" />
  </root>
</log4j:configuration>
```

Start one or more `LogStdin` applications as follows:

```
java chapter4.LogStdin chapter4/weblogic.xml
```

Make sure that log4j classes as well as *weblogic.jar* are available on the classpath. Note that *examples/resources/weblogic/* directory is not required to be on the classpath because all JNDI related information is specified through `JMSAppender` options.

Each line entered on `LogStdin` will appear on the `JMSSink` window. You can open more than one `JMSSink` window. Each line will appear on *all* the `JMSSink` windows you opened.

Setting up JMSAppender with JBoss (tested with version 3.0.1)

Running `JMSAppender` with JBossMQ, the JMS provider in JBoss, is not very different: a topic connection factory and topic must be configured. To ease our task, JBoss ships with a connection factory called "ConnectionFactory" and a topic called "topic/testTopic" already pre-configured in the JNDI namespace. These suffice for the purposes of the next example.

Before launching JMSSink on the command line make sure that the following jar files are on the classpath:

```
JBOSS/client/jboss-j2ee.jar
JBOSS/client/jnp-client.jar
JBOSS/client/jnet.jar
JBOSS/client/jbosssx-client.jar
JBOSS/client/jbossmq-client.jar
JBOSS/client/jboss-common-client.jar
JBOSS/client/concurrent.jar
```

where *JBOSS* is the name of the directory where you installed JBoss. If you intend to use configuration written in XML, then you must also add a JAXP parser to the classpath. This manual includes a JBoss specific *jndi.properties* file in the *examples/resources/jboss/* directory. The contents of this file are reproduced below.

```
java.naming.factory.initial=org.jnp.interfaces.NamingContextFactory
java.naming.provider.url=jnp://localhost:1099
java.naming.factory.url.pkgs=org.jboss.naming:org.jnp.interfaces
```

Once you have configured the classpath, start the JMSSink in a command window as follows.

```
java org.apache.log4j.net.JMSSink ConnectionFactory \
   topic/testTopic guest guest chapter4/jmssink.xml
```

Note that the command to start JMSSink with JBoss differs only in connection factory and topic names. We did not need to change the user name because by happenstance, the "guest" user is also predefined in JBoss.

Once JMSSink, our event consumer is ready, a logging event producer can be started. As in the previous example, we attach a JMSAppender to our simple application named chapter4.LogStdin. This application reads the input typed on the console line by line. Each line is then logged at the debug level. The LogStdin admits one parameter which is the path to a configuration file. The configuration file *jboss.xml,* which is listed below, creates a JMSAppender with the appropriate options. This appender is then attached to the root logger.

Example 4-4: JMSAppender configuration for JBoss *(examples/chapter4/jboss.xml)*

```
<?xml version="1.0" encoding="UTF-8" ?>
<!DOCTYPE log4j:configuration SYSTEM "log4j.dtd">
<log4j:configuration debug="true"
                xmlns:log4j='http://jakarta.apache.org/log4j/'>
```

```
<appender name="JMS" class="org.apache.log4j.net.JMSAppender">
  <param name="InitialContextFactoryName"
         value="org.jnp.interfaces.NamingContextFactory"/>
  <param name="ProviderURL" value="jnp://localhost:1099"/>
  <param name="URLPkgPrefixes"
         value="org.jboss.naming:org.jnp.interfaces"/>
  <param name="TopicConnectionFactoryBindingName"
         value="ConnectionFactory"/>
  <param name="TopicBindingName" value="topic/testTopic"/>
  <param name="UserName" value="guest"/>
  <param name="Password" value="guest"/>
  <param name="LocationInfo" value="true"/>
</appender>

<root>
  <level value ="debug"/>
  <appender-ref ref="JMS" />
</root>
</log4j:configuration>
```

Start one or more `LogStdin` applications as follows:

```
java chapter4.LogStdin chapter4/jboss.xml
```

Make sure that log4j classes as well as the aforementioned list of JBoss related files are available on the classpath. Note that *examples/resources/jboss/* directory is not required to be on the classpath because all JNDI related information is specified through the options included in the configuration file.

Each line entered on `LogStdin` will appear on the `JMSSink` window. In case you are running multiple `JMSSink` windows, then each line will be received by every sink.

Comments on JMSAppender

Transmitting a packet of information using JMS is certain to be substantially slower then sending the same packet using raw TCP sockets. JMS vendors bragging about the performance of their messaging platform tend to omit this simple fact. Guaranteed store and forward messaging comes at a hefty price. In return for increased cost, JMS messaging provides decoupling of sender and receiver. As long as the JMS provider is reachable, messages will eventually arrive at destination. However, what if the JMS server is down or simply unreachable?

According to the JMS specification, producers can mark a message as either *persistent* or *non-persistent*. The persistent delivery mode instructs the JMS provider to log the message to stable storage as part of the client's send operation, allowing the message to survive provider crashes. `JMSAppender` does not set the delivery mode of messages it produces because according to the JMS specification, the delivery mode is considered as an administered property.

Once a message reaches the JMS provider, the provider assumes the responsibility of delivering it to its destination, relieving the client from this chore. What if the JMS server is unreachable? The JMS API provides an `ExceptionListener` interface to deal with this situation. When the client runtime of the JMS provider detects a lost connection to the JMS server, it calls the `onException()` method of the registered `ExceptionListener`. Once notified of the problem, client code can attempt to reestablish the connection. According to the section 4.3.8 of the JMS specification, the provider should attempt to resolve connection problems prior to notifying the client. Up to an including log4j version 1.2.7, the `JMSAppender` does not implement the `ExceptionListener` interface. A future version of log4j may offer a more complete solution.

SMTPAppender

The `SMTPAppender` accumulates logging events in a fixed-size buffer and sends them in an e-mail when a user specified triggering event occurs. By default, the triggering event is taken as the reception of an event of level `ERROR` or higher.

The `SMTPAppender` keeps only the last **BufferSize** logging events in its cyclic buffer, throwing away older events when its buffer becomes full. The number of logging events delivered in any e-mail sent by `SMTPAppender` is upper-bounded by **BufferSize**. This keeps memory requirements bounded while still delivering the desired amount of application context.

The `SMTPAppender` relies on the JavaMail API. It has been tested with JavaMail API version 1.2. The JavaMail API requires the JavaBeans Activation Framework package. You can download the JavaMail API at *http://java.sun.com/products/-javamail/* and the JavaBeans Activation Framework at *http://java.sun.com/-beans/glasgow/jaf.html*. For your convenience, the required jar files are shipped with this manual under the *lib/* directory, respectively as *mail.jar* and *activation.jar*. Make sure to place these two jar files in the classpath before trying the following examples.

A sample application called `chapter4.EMail` takes two parameters. The first parameter is an integer corresponding to the number of logging events to generate. The second parameter is the log4j configuration file in properties or XML format. The last logging event generated by `chapter4.Email` application is always an `ERROR` event which triggers the transmission of an e-mail message.

Here is a sample configuration file you can supply to `chapter4.Email`:

Example 4-5: A sample SMTPAppender configuration file (examples/chapter4/mail1.xml)

```xml
<?xml version="1.0" encoding="UTF-8" ?>
<!DOCTYPE log4j:configuration SYSTEM "log4j.dtd">

<log4j:configuration debug="true"
                     xmlns:log4j='http://jakarta.apache.org/log4j/'>

  <appender name="EMAIL" class="org.apache.log4j.net.SMTPAppender">
    <param name="SMTPHost" value="ADDRESS-OF-YOUR-SMTP-HOST"/>
    <param name="To" value="DESTINATION1@EMAIL,
                            DESTINATION2@EMAIL"/>
    <param name="From" value="SENDER@EMAIL"/>
    <layout class="org.apache.log4j.PatternLayout">
      <param name="ConversionPattern" value="%d %-5p %c - %m%n"/>
    </layout>
  </appender>

  <root>
    <level value ="debug"/>
    <appender-ref ref="EMAIL" />
  </root>
</log4j:configuration>
```

Before trying out `chapter4.Email` application with the above configuration file, you must set the **SMTPHost, To** and **From** options to values appropriate for your environment. Once you have set the proper values, execute the following command:

```
java chapter4.EMail 300 chapter4/mail.xml
```

The chosen recipient should see an e-mail message containing 300 logging events formatted by `PatternLayout`.

In another configuration file *mail2.xml* included under *chaper4/examples/* directory, the values for the **SMTPHost, To** and **From** options are determined by variable substitution. Here is the relevant part of *mail2.xml*.

```xml
  <appender name="EMAIL" class="org.apache.log4j.net.SMTPAppender">
    <param name="SMTPHost" value="${smtpHost}"/>
    <param name="To" value="${to}"/>
    <param name="From" value="${from}"/>
    <layout class="org.apache.log4j.HTMLLayout"/>
  </appender>
```

You can supply the various values on the command line:

```
java -Dfrom=source@xyz.com -Dto=recipient@xyz.com
  -DsmtpHost=some_smtp_host chapter4.EMail 10000 chapter4/mail2.xml
```

Be sure to replace with the correct values appropriate for your environment.

Given that the default size of the cyclic buffer is 512, the recipient should see an e-mail message containing 512 events conveniently formatted in an HTML table. Note that this run of the `chapter4.Email` application generated 10'000 events of which only the last 512 were included in the e-mail.

The various options for `SMTPAppender` are summarized in the following table.

Option Name	Type	Description
SMTPHost	String	The host name of the SMTP server. This parameter is mandatory.
To	String	The e-mail address of the recipient. Multiple recipients can be specified by separating each recipient with a comma.
From	String	The stated originator of the e-mail messages sent by SMTPAppender.
BufferSize	int	The BufferSize option takes a positive integer representing the maximum number of logging events to collect in a cyclic buffer. When the BufferSize is reached, oldest events are deleted as new events are added to the buffer. The default size of the cyclic buffer is 512.
EvaluatorClass	String	The EvaluatorClass option takes a string value representing the name of the class implementing the TriggeringEventEvaluator interface. A corresponding object will be instantiated and assigned as the triggering event evaluator for the SMTPAppender. In the absence of this option, SMTPAppender is assigned a default evaluator which triggers e-mail transmission as a response to any event of level ERROR or higher.

LocationInfo	boolean	The LocationInfo option takes a boolean value. If true, then the events placed in the cyclic buffer will include location information. By default no location information is included in the buffered events.
Threshold	Level	See AppenderSkeleton options.

By default, the SMTPAppender will initiate the transmission of an e-mail message as a response to an event of level ERROR or higher. However, it is possible to override this default behavior by providing a custom implementation of the TriggeringEventEvaluator interface. This interface contains a single method named isTriggeringEvent().

```
package org.apache.log4j.spi;

public interface TriggeringEventEvaluator {
  public boolean isTriggeringEvent(LoggingEvent event);
}
```

The SMTPAppender submits each incoming event to its evaluator by calling isTriggeringEvent() method in order to check whether the event should trigger an e-mail or just be placed in the cyclic buffer. The SMTPAppender contains one and only one evaluator object. This object may possess its own state. For illustrative purposes, the CounterBasedTEE class listed next, implements a triggering policy whereby every 1024th event triggers an e-mail message.

Example 4-6: A TriggeringEventEvaluator implementation that triggers every 1024th event (examples/chapter4/ CounterBasedTEE.java)

```
package chapter4;
import org.apache.log4j.spi.TriggeringEventEvaluator;
import org.apache.log4j.spi.LoggingEvent;

public class CounterBasedTEE implements TriggeringEventEvaluator {
  int counter = 0;
  static int LIMIT = 1024;
  public boolean isTriggeringEvent(LoggingEvent event) {
    counter++;
    if(counter == LIMIT) {
      counter = 0;
      return true;
    } else {
      return false;
    }
  }
}
```

Setting the `EvaluatorClass` option of `SMTPAppender` instructs it to use a custom evaluator. The next configuration file attaches a `SMTPAppender` to the root logger. This appender has a buffer size of 2048 and uses a `CounterBasedTEE` instance as its triggering event evaluator.

Example 4-7: SMTPAppender with custom evaluator and buffer size (examples/chapter4/mail3.xml)

```
<?xml version="1.0" encoding="UTF-8" ?>
<!DOCTYPE log4j:configuration SYSTEM "log4j.dtd">

<log4j:configuration debug="true"
                xmlns:log4j='http://jakarta.apache.org/log4j/'>

  <appender name="EMAIL" class="org.apache.log4j.net.SMTPAppender">
    <param name="EvaluatorClass" value="chapter4.CounterBasedTEE"/>
    <param name="SMTPHost" value="${smtpHost}"/>
    <param name="BufferSize" value="2048"/>
    <param name="To" value="${to}"/>
    <param name="From" value="${from}"/>
    <layout class="org.apache.log4j.HTMLLayout"/>
  </appender>

  <root>
    <level value ="debug"/>
    <appender-ref ref="EMAIL" />
  </root>
</log4j:configuration>
```

AsyncAppender

The `AsyncAppender` logs events asynchronously. It uses a bounded queue to store events. The `AsyncAppender.append()` method immediately returns after placing events in the bounded queue. The events accumulated in the bounded queue are served by an internal thread called the *dispatcher* thread. While the bounded queue is not empty, the dispatcher thread will continuously remove the oldest event in the queue and dispatch it to all the appenders attached to the `AsyncAppender`. Zero or more appenders can be attached to `AsyncAppender`. Appending to `AsyncAppender` is non-blocking as long as the bounded queue is not full. If however the queue is full, then `AsyncAppender.append()` will not return until free space becomes available. The dispatcher thread will free space, one event at a time. It will remove the oldest event at the bottom of the queue, dispatch it to each attached appender, wait for them to finish appending, and only then serve the next event from the queue.

The `AsyncAppender` does not improve logging throughput. On the contrary, non-negligible number of CPU cycles are spent managing the bounded queue and synchronizing the dispatcher thread with various client threads. Thus, while logging each event will take a little longer to complete, appending those events will hopefully take place at times where other threads are idle, either waiting for new input to process or blocked on I/O intensive operations. Thus, I/O bound applications will benefit from asynchronous logging while CPU bound applications will not.

Given that AsyncAppender is a composite appender containing other appenders, it can only be configured by DOMConfigurator. In configuration files, an appender is attached to an AsyncAppender by reference. Once configured, AsyncAppender can be attached to a logger like any other appender, as the next sample configuration file *async.xml* illustrates:

Example 4-8: AsyncAppender with two attached appenders (examples/chapter4/async.xml)

```
<?xml version="1.0" encoding="UTF-8" ?>
<!DOCTYPE log4j:configuration SYSTEM "log4j.dtd">

<log4j:configuration debug="true"
                     xmlns:log4j='http://jakarta.apache.org/log4j/'>

  <appender name="ASYNC" class="org.apache.log4j.AsyncAppender">
    <param name="BufferSize" value="256"/>
    <appender-ref ref="FILE" />
    <appender-ref ref="CONSOLE" />
  </appender>

  <appender name="CONSOLE" class="org.apache.log4j.ConsoleAppender">
    <layout class="org.apache.log4j.PatternLayout">
      <param name="ConversionPattern" value="%d [%t] %-5p %c - %m%n"/>
    </layout>
  </appender>

  <appender name="FILE" class="org.apache.log4j.FileAppender">
    <param name="File" value="sample.log"/>
    <param name="Append" value="false"/>
    <layout class="org.apache.log4j.PatternLayout">
      <param name="ConversionPattern" value="%d [%t] %-5p %c - %m%n"/>
    </layout>
  </appender>

  <root>
    <level value="debug"/>
    <appender-ref ref="ASYNC" />
  </root>
</log4j:configuration>
```

NOTE Given its composite nature, the AsyncAppender can only be configured using DOMConfigurator.

The various options for `AsyncAppender` are summarized in the table below.

Option Name	Type	Description
BufferSize	`int`	The `BufferSize` option takes a positive integer representing the maximum number of logging events that can be buffered in the internal queue. The default size of the buffer is 128.
LocationInfo	`boolean`	The LocationInfo option takes a boolean value. If set to true, `AsyncAppender` will extract location information prior to inserting the event in the queue. As a result, events will carry the correct location information even if logged asynchronously. Otherwise, events are likely to contain the wrong location information, assuming such information is present in the output format. Location information extraction is comparatively slow and should be avoided unless performance is not a concern. Given that `AsyncAppender` exists for the sole purpose of improving performance, setting LocationInfo defeats the rationale for using `AsyncAppender`. By default no location information extracted prior to insertion in the queue.
Threshold	`Level`	See `AppenderSkeleton` options.

Handling Errors

Appenders can delegate the processing of error conditions to an object implementing the `org.apache.log4j.spi.ErrorHandler` interface. By default, the `AppenderSkeleton` sets the error handler to an `OnceOnlyErrorHandler` which prints a single warning message on the console – the first error is reported while subsequent errors are ignored. The `ErrorHandler` interface is listed below:

```
package org.apache.log4j.spi;

import org.apache.log4j.Appender;
import org.apache.log4j.Logger;

public interface ErrorHandler extends OptionHandler {

  void setLogger(Logger logger);
  void error(String message, Exception e, int errorCode);
  void error(String message);
  void error(String message, Exception e, int errorCode,
             LoggingEvent event);

  void setAppender(Appender appender);
  void setBackupAppender(Appender appender);
}
```

All appenders derived from `AppenderSkeleton` contain one and only one `Er-rorHandler`. Appenders call one of the `error()` methods of their error handler to signal an error condition. The invocation of the `setAppender()` method informs the error handler of the primary appender it is associated with. The `set-BackupAppender()` associates a backup appender with the error handler. Not all error handlers make use of the backup appender. The `setLogger` method, which should have been better called the `addLogger`, adds a logger to search for when reacting to error conditions. Indeed, some error handlers will detach the primary appender from the loggers and replace it with the backup appender.

The `OnceOnlyErrorHandler` does not make use of any of this information. It just prints the first error message it receives, ignoring following errors. The `Fall-backErrorHandler` in package `org.apache.log4j.varia`, implements a more sophisticated policy. In response to an error in the primary appender, it detaches it from the loggers where it is attached and replaces it with the fallback appender.

In configuration files, the error handler of an appender can be configured with the `<errorHandler>` element. This element was formally introduced in the previous chapter on page 66. It has a mandatory *class* attribute which specifies fully qualified name of the error handler implementation to be associated with the containing appender. It may contain `<param>` elements to be passed on as parameters to the error handler. The `FallbackErrorHandler` does not make use of `<param>` elements. The `<root-ref>` element and the `<logger-ref>` elements refer to loggers where the primary appender is attached to. The `<appender-ref>` element refers to the appender serving as backup in case of failure with the primary appender.

The next configuration file illustrates `FallbackErrorHandler` usage.

Example 4-9: Sample FallbackErrorHandler configuration (examples/chapter4/-fallback1.xml)

```
<?xml version="1.0" encoding="UTF-8" ?>
<!DOCTYPE log4j:configuration SYSTEM "log4j.dtd">

<log4j:configuration debug="true"
                     xmlns:log4j="http://jakarta.apache.org/log4j/">

  <appender name="PRIMARY" class="org.apache.log4j.FileAppender">
    <errorHandler class="org.apache.log4j.varia.FallbackErrorHandler">
      <root-ref/>
      <appender-ref ref="FALLBACK" />
    </errorHandler>

    <param name="File" value="/xyz/x.log" />
    <layout class="org.apache.log4j.PatternLayout">
      <param name="ConversionPattern" value="%-5p %c{2} - %m%n"/>
    </layout>
  </appender>

  <appender name="FALLBACK" class="org.apache.log4j.FileAppender">
    <param name="File" value="fallback.log" />
    <param name="Append" value="false" />
    <layout class="org.apache.log4j.PatternLayout">
      <param name="ConversionPattern" value="--%d %p %t %c - %m%n"/>
    </layout>
  </appender>

  <root>
    <level value="debug" />
    <appender-ref ref="PRIMARY" />
  </root>
</log4j:configuration>
```

In the above configuration file, a `FileAppender` named "PRIMARY" is attached to the root logger. This appender's error handler, of type `FallbackErrorHandler`, refers to a `FileAppender` named "FALLBACK". The `<root-ref>` element indicates that the containing appender is attached to the root logger. This information is used by the fallback error handler to locate the loggers where the primary appender is attached.

Assuming that the */xyz/* directory does not exist, the `FileAppender` will not be able to open the */xyz/x.log* file and will fail before writing a single message. However, it will call its error handler, which will replace the failing "PRMARY" appender with the "FALLBACK" appender.

You can see the `FallbackErrorHandler` in action by issuing the following command.

```
java chapter4.EventGenerator 10 chapter4/fallback1.xml
```

The messages appearing on the console should show the failure of the primary appender and its replacement with its backup. Moreover, none of the generated events will be lost. They will all appear in the file *fallback.log*.

Writing your own Appender

You can easily write your appender by sub-classing `AppenderSkeleton`. It handles support for filters, layouts, append threshold among other functionality shared by most appenders. The derived class only needs to implement a small number of methods, namely `append(LoggingEvent)`, `close()` and `requiresLayout()`.

The `CountingConsoleAppender`, which we list next, appends a limited number of incoming events on the console. It shuts down after the limit is reached.

Example 4-10: A sample appender that outputs a limited number of events on the console(examples/chapter4/CountingConsoleAppender.java)

```
package chapter4;

import org.apache.log4j.AppenderSkeleton;
import org.apache.log4j.spi.LoggingEvent;
import org.apache.log4j.spi.ErrorCode;
import org.apache.log4j.Layout;
import org.apache.log4j.helpers.LogLog;


public class CountingConsoleAppender extends AppenderSkeleton {

    int counter = 0;
    int limit = 16;

    public CountingConsoleAppender() { }
    public void setLimit(int limit) { this.limit = limit; }
    public int getLimit() { return limit; }

    public void append(LoggingEvent event) {

      if(this.layout == null) {
        errorHandler.error("No layout set for the appender named ["
                        + name+"].", null,  ErrorCode.MISSING_LAYOUT);
        return;
      }
```

```
  if(counter >= limit) {
    errorHandler.error("Counter limit reached in ["+ getName()
                       +"] appender", null, ErrorCode.WRITE_FAILURE);
    return;
  }

  // output the events as formatted by our layout
  System.out.print(this.layout.format(event));

  // if our layout does not handle exceptions, we have to do it.
  if(layout.ignoresThrowable()) {
    String[] t = event.getThrowableStrRep();
    if (t != null) {
     int len = t.length;
     for(int i = 0;  i < len;  i++) {
       System.out.println(t[i]);
     }
    }
  }
  // prepare for next event
  counter++;
}

public void close() {
  if(this.closed) // closed is defined in AppenderSkeleton
    return;
  this.closed = true;
}

public boolean requiresLayout() { return true; }
}
```

This custom appender illustrates a number of points.

- All options that follow the setter/getter JavaBeans conventions are handled transparently. However, in case of interdependency between options, they can be activated concomitantly within the `activateOptions` method. See the source code `FileAppender`, `JMSAppender` or `SMTPAppender` for examples.

- The `AppenderSkeleton.doAppend`[20] method invokes the `append()` method of its derived classes where actual output operations occur. It is in this method that appenders format events by invoking their layouts. In case their layout ignores exceptions, derived appenders are also responsible for output-

---

[20] See the begging of this chapter for a discussion on `AppenderSkeleton.doAppend` method.

ting the exception included in the event. The derived appender must also call its error handler in case of errors.

- Derived appenders must set the value of the `closed` field (defined in `AppenderSkeleton`) to true when their `close()` method is invoked.

- Derived appenders requiring a layout must return true in their `requiresLayout()` method.

The `CountingConsoleAppender` can be configured like any appender. See sample file *examples/chapter4/countingConsole.xml* for an example. Our custom appender also handles error conditions. Execute the following command to see our custom appender being replaced by a regular `ConsoleAppender` after our self-imposed limit is reached.

```
java chapter4.EventGenerator 20 chapter4/fallback2.xml
```

5

> TCP implementations will follow a general principle of
> robustness: be conservative in what you do, be liberal in
> what you accept from others.
>
> —JON POSTEL, RFC 793

While appenders are responsible for writing logging output to an appender dependent device, layouts are responsible for the format of the output. In case you were
wondering, layouts have nothing to do with large estates in Florida. The format()
method in the Layout class takes in a LoggingEvent and returns a String. A
synopsis of the Layout class is shown below.

```
public abstract class Layout implements OptionHandler {

    // Derived classes need to implement their own formatting strategy.
    abstract public String format(LoggingEvent event);

    public String getContentType() { return "text/plain"; }
    public String getHeader() { return null; }
    public String getFooter() { return null; }
    abstract public boolean ignoresThrowable();
}
```

Actually, except for the omission of comments and the usual paraphernalia, the
above *is* the complete Layout implementation. Honest. The Texan developer from
Texas might exclaim: it just takes two methods to implement a layout!!?

Writing your own Layout

Let us implement a functional layout which prints the time elapsed since the start
of the application, the level of the logging event, the caller thread between brackets, its logger, a dash followed by the event message and a new line. Sample output
might look like:

```
10489 DEBUG [main] com.marsupial.Pouch - Hello world.
```

Here is a possible implementation authored by the Texan developer:

```
package chapter5;
import org.apache.log4j.Layout;
import org.apache.log4j.spi.LoggingEvent;

public class MyLayout1 extends Layout {

  public MyLayout1() {}
  public void activateOptions() {}

  public String format(LoggingEvent event) {
    StringBuffer sbuf = new StringBuffer(128);
    sbuf.append(event.timeStamp - event.getStartTime());
    sbuf.append(" ");
    sbuf.append(event.level.toString());
    sbuf.append(" [");
    sbuf.append(event.getThreadName());
    sbuf.append("] ");
    sbuf.append(event.getLoggerName());
    sbuf.append(" - ");
    sbuf.append(event.getRenderedMessage());
    sbuf.append(LINE_SEP);
    return sbuf.toString();
  }

  // MyLayout1 ignores any throwable contained in the event. Thus, it
  // is the responsibility of the containing appender to handle the
  // throwable, if any such throwable exists.
  public boolean ignoresThrowable() {
    return true;
  }
}
```

Note that the Layout class implements the OptionHandler interface. Since My-
Layout1 does not have any options, its activateOptions method is empty. The
marginally more interesting format method begins by instantiating a String-
Buffer. It proceeds by adding various fields of the event parameter. The Texan
from Texas[21] was careful to print the rendered form of the message and not its object form. This allows for object rendering to kick-in in case there are registered
ObjectRenderer instances. In the previous listing of the Layout class, we had
omitted the class static LINE_SEP field which is simply assigned the value returned by System.getProperty("line. separator") method. After adding
system dependent line separator character(s), the format method returns the string

---

[21] This character "also" appears in Joseph Heller's novel *Catch-22*.

buffer as a String. The `format` method ignores any eventual exceptions contained in the event, leaving the task of handling throwables to the containing appender.

Custom layouts are configured as any other layout, as shown below.

Example 5-1: Configuring a custom layout (examples/chapter5/mylayout1.xml)

```
<?xml version="1.0" encoding="UTF-8" ?>
<!DOCTYPE log4j:configuration SYSTEM "log4j.dtd">

<log4j:configuration xmlns:log4j='http://jakarta.apache.org/log4j/'>

  <appender name="CONSOLE" class="org.apache.log4j.ConsoleAppender">
    <layout class="chapter5.MyLayout1"/>
  </appender>

  <root>
    <level value="debug"/>
    <appender-ref ref="CONSOLE" />
  </root>
</log4j:configuration>
```

The sample application `chapter5.Sample` configures log4j with the configuration script supplied as parameter and then logs a debug message, followed by an error message containing an exception. See *examples/chapter5/Sample.java* for precise details.

Executing the command

```
java chapter5.Sample chapter5/mylayout1.xml
```

will yield the following output on the console:

```
0 DEBUG [main] chapter5.Sample - First message
11 WARN [main] chapter5.Sample - Nothing is wrong, just testing.
java.lang.Exception: Just a test.
        at chapter5.Sample.main(Sample.java:34)
```

That was simple enough. The skeptic Pyrrho of Elea might ask: how about a layout with options? The reader shall perhaps[22] find a slightly modified version of our custom layout in *MyLayout2.java*. She will discover that adding an option to a layout is as simple as declaring a setter method for the option. See also *chapter5/mylayout2.xml* for a configuration example.

---

[22] Pyrrho insists that nothing is certain except perhaps uncertainty itself, which is by no means certain either.

PatternLayout

Although easy, users rarely have to write a custom layout. Indeed, log4j ships with a flexible layout called `PatternLayout`. As all layouts, `PatternLayout` takes in a `LoggingEvent` and returns a `String`. However, the returned `String` can be modified at will by tweaking its *conversion pattern*. The conversion pattern of `PatternLayout` is closely related to the conversion pattern of the `printf()` function in the C programming language. A conversion pattern is composed of *literal text* and format control expressions called *conversion specifiers*. You are free to insert any literal text within the conversion pattern.

Each conversion specifier starts with a percent sign (%) and is followed by optional *format modifiers* and a *conversion character*. The conversion character controls the type of data to use, e.g. logger name, level, date, thread name. The format modifiers control such things as field width, padding, and left or right justification. The following is a simple example.

Example 5-2 Sample PatternLayout usage. (*examples/chapter5/PatternSample.java*)

```
package chapter5;

import org.apache.log4j.Logger;
import org.apache.log4j.PatternLayout;
import org.apache.log4j.ConsoleAppender;

public class PatternSample {

  static public void main(String[] args) throws Exception {
    Logger rootLogger = Logger.getRootLogger();
    PatternLayout layout = new PatternLayout("%-5p [%t]: %m%n");
    ConsoleAppender appender = new ConsoleAppender(layout);
    rootLogger.addAppender(appender);

    rootLogger.debug("Message 1");
    rootLogger.warn("Message 2");
  }
}
```

The conversion pattern is set to be "**%-5p [%t]: %m%n**". Running *PatternSample* will yield the following output on the console.

```
DEBUG [main]: Message 1
WARN  [main]: Message 2
```

Note that in the conversion pattern "%-5p [%t]: %m%n" there is no explicit separator between literal text and conversion specifiers. When parsing a conversion pattern, `PatternLayout` is capable of differentiating between literal text (space char-

characters, the brackets, colon character) and conversion specifiers. In the example above, the conversion specifier **%-5p** means the priority (i.e. level) of the logging event should be left justified to a width of five characters. Format specifiers will be explained in a short moment.

The recognized conversion characters are listed in the table below.

Conversion Character	Effect
c	Outputs the category[23] (logger) of the logging event. The category conversion specifier can be optionally followed by *precision specifier*, that is a decimal constant within braces. If a precision specifier is given, then only the corresponding number of *right most* components of the logger name will be printed. For example, for the logger name "a.b.c" the pattern %c{2} will output "b.c". By default the logger name is printed in full.
C	Outputs the fully qualified class name of the caller issuing the logging request. This conversion specifier can be optionally followed by *precision specifier*, that is a decimal constant in braces. If a precision specifier is given, then only the corresponding number of right most components of the class name will be printed. By default, the class name is printed in full. For example, for the class name "org.apache.xyz.SomeClass", the pattern %C{1} will output "SomeClass".
d	Outputs the date of the logging event. The date conversion specifier may be followed by a *date format specifier* enclosed between braces. For example, %d{dd MMM yyyy HH:mm:ss} or %d{HH:mm:ss,SSS}. In the absence of a date format specifier, ISO8601 format is assumed by default. The date format specifier admits the same syntax as the time pattern string of the `java.text.SimpleDateFormat`. Although part of the standard JDK, the performance of `SimpleDateFormat` is quite poor. For better results it is recommended to use the log4j date formatters. These can be specified using one of the strings "ABSOLUTE", "DATE" and "ISO8601" for respectively `AbsoluteTimeDateFormat`, `DateTimeDateFormat` and `ISO8601DateFormat`. For

[23] The names category and priority and their respective conversion characters are retained for historical reasons. Conversion specifiers will be considerably improved and expanded in future log4j versions.

	example, %d{ISO8601} or %d{ABSOLUTE}. These dedicated date formatters perform substantially better than `SimpleDateFormat`.
F	Outputs the file name where the logging request was issued.
l	Outputs location information for the caller issuing the logging request. The location information depends on the JVM implementation but usually consists of the fully qualified name of the calling method followed by the caller's source file and line number. The location information can be very useful. However, its extraction can be extremely slow. Its use should be avoided unless execution speed is not an issue.
L	Outputs the line number from where the logging request was issued, that is the caller's line number.
m	Outputs the application supplied message associated with the logging event.
M	Outputs the method name where the logging request was issued.
n	Outputs the platform dependent line separator character or characters. This conversion character offers practically the same performance as using non-portable line separator strings such as "\n", or "\r\n". Thus, it is the preferred way of specifying a line separator.
p	Outputs the priority, a.k.a. the level, of the logging event.
r	Outputs the number of milliseconds elapsed since the start of the application until the creation of the logging event.
t	Outputs the name of the thread that generated the logging event.
x	Outputs the NDC (nested diagnostic context) associated with the thread that generated the logging event. The NDC will be discussed in Chapter 7.
X	Outputs the MDC (mapped diagnostic context) associated with the thread that generated the logging event. The X conversion character *must* be followed by a key placed between braces, as in %X{clientNumber} where `clientNumber` is the key. The corresponding value in the MDC will be output. The MDC will be discussed in Chapter 7.
%	The sequence %% outputs a single percent sign.

WARNING On certain platforms, generating the caller class information can be excruciatingly slow. Thus, the use of the C, F, l, L, and M conversion characters should be avoided unless execution speed is not an issue.

By default the relevant information is output as is. However, with the aid of *format modifiers* it is possible to change the minimum field width, the maximum field width and justification. The optional format modifier is placed between the percent sign and the conversion character.

The first optional format modifier is the *left justification flag* which is just the minus (-) character. The second optional modifier is the *minimum field width* modifier. This is a decimal constant that represents the minimum number of characters to output. If the data item requires fewer characters, it is padded on either the left or the right until the minimum width is reached. The default is to pad on the left (right justify) but you can specify right padding with the left justification flag. The padding character is space. If the data item is larger than the minimum field width, the field is expanded to accommodate the data. The value is not truncated.

This behavior can be changed using the *maximum field width* modifier which is designated by a period followed by a decimal constant. If the data item is longer than the maximum field, then the extra characters are removed from the *beginning* of the data item and not from the end. For example, it the maximum field width is eight and the data item is ten characters long, then the first two characters of the data item are dropped. This behavior deviates from the `printf` function in C where truncation is done from the end.

The table below gives examples of various format modifiers for the category conversion specifier.

Format modifier	left justify	minimum width	maximum width	comment
%20c	false	20	None	Left pad with spaces if the logger name is less than 20 characters long.
%-20c	true	20	None	Right pad with spaces if the logger name is less than 20 characters long.
%.30c	NA	none	30	Truncate from the beginning if the logger name is longer than 30 characters.
%20.30c	false	20	30	Left pad with spaces if the logger name is shorter than 20 characters. However, if logger name is longer than 30 characters, then truncate from the beginning.

%-20.30c	true	20	30	Right pad with spaces if the logger name is shorter than 20 characters. However, if logger name is longer than 30 characters, then truncate from the beginning.

Below are some examples of conversion patterns.

ConversionPattern: `%r [%t] %-5p %c - %m%n`

Sample output:

```
100 [main] INFO  com.marsupial.Pouch - Hi. I am from Australia.
110 [main] DEBUG com.marsupial.Pouch - Hi again.
120 [main] WARN  com.marsupial.Gopher - I must dig further.
```

Here is another one: `%-6r [%10.10t] %-5p %20.20c %x - %m%n`

Sample output:

```
0        [     main] DEBUG      chapter5.Sample  - First message
10       [     main] WARN       chapter5.Sample  - Nothing is wrong.
```

The relative time is right padded when less than 6 digits, thread name is right padded when less than 10 characters and truncated when longer. The logger name is left padded when shorter than 20 characters but truncated when longer.

The synopsis for the `PatternLayout` is inspired from "C – a Software Engineering Approach," ISBN 0-387-97389-3, a highly recommended book by Peter A. Darnell and Philip E. Margolis.

XMLLayout

The `XMLLayout` produces a stream of log events in a fixed format. More specifically, the output of the `XMLLayout` consists of a series of `<log4j:event>` elements as defined in the *log4j.dtd*. It does not produce a completely well-formed XML file. The output is designed to be included as an external entity in a separate file in order to form a correct XML file.

For example, if *abc.log* is the name of the file where the `XMLLayout` results go, then the following file includes it as an external entity:

```
<?xml version="1.0" ?>

<!DOCTYPE log4j:eventSet SYSTEM "log4j.dtd"
          [<!ENTITY data SYSTEM "abc.log">]>

<log4j:eventSet version="1.2"
                xmlns:log4j="http://jakarta.apache.org/log4j/">
  &data;
</log4j:eventSet>
```

This approach enforces the independence of the XMLLayout and its containing appender.

The version attribute helps components to correctly interpret output generated by XMLLayout. The value of this attribute should be "1.1" for output generated by log4j versions prior to log4j 1.2 and "1.2" for release 1.2 and later.

The XMLLayout admits a single option LocationInfo:

Option Name	Type	Description
LocationInfo	boolean	The LocationInfo option takes a boolean value. If true, the output includes the caller's location information. By default no location information is included.

A logging event of level WARN, issued by a logger named "chapter5.Sample" containing the message "Hello World." would be formatted as follows:

```
<log4j:event logger="chapter5.Sample" timestamp="1025013672760"
level="WARN" thread="main">
<log4j:message><![CDATA[Hello world.]]></log4j:message>
</log4j:event>
```

Like most XML output, the output of the XMLLayout is usually presented to the user in a different form after further transformation. The chainsaw tool, part of the log4j project, can read files produced by XMLLayout and present them to the user in an easily readable Swing table.

HTMLLayout

The HTMLLayout outputs events in a fixed format table. Each row of the table corresponds to an event. Each row is divided into five columns: Time, Thread, Level, Logger and Message corresponding to member fields of the logging event. Sample configuration files are included in the *examples/chapter5/* folder.

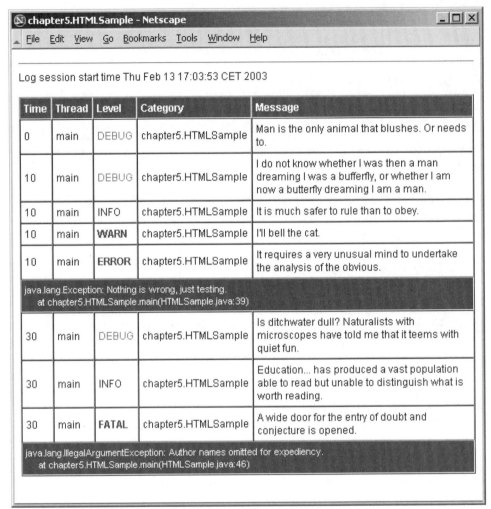

Figure 5-1: Sample output of HTMLLayout

The HTMLLayout admits two options, namely **LocationInfo** and **Title**.

Option Name	Type	Description
LocationInfo	boolean	The **LocationInfo** option takes a boolean value. If true, the output includes the caller's location information in an additional "File:Line" column. By default no location information is included.
Title	String	The title of the generated HTML page.

6

CUSTOM FILTERS

*Have lots of ideas and throw away the bad ones. You
aren't going to have good ideas unless you have lots of
ideas and some sort of principle of selection.*
—LINUS PAULING

As we have seen, log4j has several built-in ways for filtering log requests, including the repository-wide filter, logger-level filter and appender thresholds. These
provide high performance filtering for the most commonly encountered cases. To
deal with more specialized cases, log4j offers the generic yet powerful mechanism
of *custom filters*. These are largely inspired from Linux ipchains or iptables as they
are called in more recent Linux kernels. Customs filters are based on ternary logic
allowing them to be assembled or *chained* together to compose an arbitrarily complex filtering policy. Hereto, filters have been an under documented and underem-
ployed log4j feature.

Custom filter classes must derive from the `org.apache.log4j.spi.Filter`
class.

```
package org.apache.log4j.spi;

public abstract class Filter implements OptionHandler {

  // point to the next filter in the chain, can be null.
  public Filter next;

  public static final int DENY = -1;
  public static final int NEUTRAL = 0;
  public static final int ACCEPT  = 1;

  // a do nothing default implementation
  public void activateOptions() {}

  // The returned value must be one of DENY, NEUTRAL or ACCEPT.
  abstract public int decide(LoggingEvent event);
}
```

Filter chains

This abstract class assumes that filters be organized in a linear chain. Its member field `next` points to the next filter in the chain, or `null` if there are no further filters in the chain. Figure 6-1 depicts a sample filter chain consisting of three filters.

Figure 6-1: A sample filter chain

Custom filters are based on ternary logic. The `decide(LoggingEvent)` method of each filter is called in sequence. This method returns one of the integer constants `DENY`, `NEUTRAL` or `ACCEPT`. If the returned value is `DENY`, then the log event is dropped immediately without consulting the remaining filters. If the value returned is `NEUTRAL`, then the next filter in the chain is consulted. If there are no further filters to consult, then the logging event is processed normally. If the returned value is `ACCEPT`, then the logging event is processed immediately skipping the remaining filters.

Up to and including log4j version 1.2, filters can only added to `Appender` instances. By adding custom filters to an appender you can filter events by various criteria, such as the contents of the log message, the contents of the NDC, the time of day or any other part of the logging event. Log4j ships with several sample filters in the `org.apache.log4j.varia` package. The `StringMatchFilter` filters events according to the contents of the message, `LevelMatchFilter` filters events by level, `LevelRangeFilter` by a range of levels, and the `DenyAllFilter`, usually placed at the end of a filter chain, denies all messages.

Below we list a filter chain that rejects any message that contains the strings "hot cakes" or "CPU cycles."

Example 6-1: Sample filter chain denying events containing the messages "hot cakes" or "CPU cycles."

```
<filter class="org.apache.log4j.varia.StringMatchFilter">
  <param name="StringToMatch" value="hot cakes" />
  <param name="AcceptOnMatch" value="false" />
</filter>
  <filter class="org.apache.log4j.varia.StringMatchFilter">
  <param name="StringToMatch" value="CPU cycles" />
  <param name="AcceptOnMatch" value="false" />
</filter>
```

The `AcceptOnMatch` attribute of `StringMatchFilter` determines the action to be taken when a string match occurs. If `AcceptOnMatch` attribute is set to true, then the filter returns the value `ACCEPT` upon a match. Otherwise, that is if `AcceptOnMatch` attribute is set to false, then the filter returns the value `DENY` upon a match. If there is no match, then the value `NEUTRAL` is returned (regardless of the value of `AcceptOnMatch` attribute).

A given filter chain can only be attached to a given appender. Moreover, in configuration files, filter chains can only be expressed in XML format. Refer to the *examples/chapter6/filter1.xml* for a complete filter chain example. Its filter chain is geared towards the sample application `chapter6.Sample1` which incidentally includes log statements containing the strings "hot cakes" and "CPU cycles."

The next filter chain accepts events containing the string "teacher" as well as all events of level info.

Example 6-2: Incomplete filter chain accepting events containing the messages "teacher" or events of level INFO.

```
<filter class="org.apache.log4j.varia.StringMatchFilter">
  <param name="StringToMatch" value="teacher" />
  <param name="AcceptOnMatch" value="true" />
</filter>
<filter class="org.apache.log4j.varia.LevelMatchFilter">
  <param name="LevelToMatch" value="info" />
  <param name="AcceptOnMatch" value="true" />
</filter>
```

Contrary to the previous filter chain, instead of denying events on match, this chain accepts events when a match occurs. This filter chain is incorporated in the configuration script *filter2.xml*. Applying it to the *chapter6.Sample1* application you should notice that not only are the designated events allowed to pass through, but so are all other events. Indeed, the filter chain in Example 6-2 is incomplete because it lets certain events pass through but does not specify the events to block. At the end of the chain, events that have been neither rejected nor accepted are processed normally – they are implicitly accepted. The following filter chain accepts events containing the string "teacher" as well as all events of level INFO. However, it denies all other events not matching these two criteria.

Example 6-3 Complete filter chain accepting events containing the messages "teacher" or events of level INFO and denying all other events.

```
<filter class="org.apache.log4j.varia.StringMatchFilter">
  <param name="StringToMatch" value="teacher" />
  <param name="AcceptOnMatch" value="true" />
</filter>
```

```
<filter class="org.apache.log4j.varia.LevelMatchFilter">
  <param name="LevelToMatch" value="info" />
  <param name="AcceptOnMatch" value="true" />
</filter>
```

`<filter class="org.apache.log4j.varia.DenyAllFilter"/>`

This filter chain differs from the previous one only by the addition of a `DenyAll-Filter` at the end of the chain. Typically, chains containing a series of "accepting" filters are terminated by a `DenyAllFilter`. The above filter chain is incorporated in the configuration script *filter3.xml*.

Configuration files in properties format do not support filter chains. There are no plans to add such support in the future. In the next version of log4j, the set of available filters will be widened and each individual filter retrofitted with the ability to act on negative matches (mismatches) whereas currently shipped filters can only act on positive matches.

Writing your own filter

The set of filters shipped with log4j is rather basic. Fortunately, writing your own custom filter is as easy as extending the `Filter` class. This involves the implementation of the `decide(LoggingEvent)` method and a getter/setter method pair for each of your filter's options.

Repeat logs, i.e. logging events carrying exactly the same message, are a commonplace phenomenon. Nestor, a wise and resolute java developer, tackles the repeat log problem with `RepeatFilter`:

Example 6-4: RepeatFilter removes repeat messages (examples/chapter6/RepeatFilter.java)

```java
package chapter6;
import org.apache.log4j.spi.Filter;
import org.apache.log4j.spi.LoggingEvent;

public class RepeatFilter extends Filter {
  String lastMessage;
  int repeatCount = 0;
  int toleratedRepeats = 0;

  public int getToleratedRepeats() {
    return toleratedRepeats;
  }
  public void setToleratedRepeats(int toleratedRepeats) {
    this.toleratedRepeats = toleratedRepeats;
  }
```

```
public int decide(LoggingEvent event) {
  // get the rendered (String) form of the message
  String msg = event.getRenderedMessage();

  if(msg == null)
    return Filter.NEUTRAL;

  if(msg.equals(lastMessage)) {
    repeatCount++;
  } else {
    repeatCount = 0;
  }

  lastMessage = msg;

  if(repeatCount > toleratedRepeats) {
    return Filter.DENY;
  } else {
    return Filter.NEUTRAL;
  }
}
}
```

The decide method of RepeatFilter checks whether the current event contains the same message as the message contained in the previous event. If the messages are the same, the repeatCount variable is incremented; otherwise it is set to zero. The decide method returns the value NEUTRAL if the current event is not a repeat or if the number of detected repeats is lower than the number of tolerated repeats, as specified by the **ToleratedRepeats** option. The decide method returns the value DENY only in case the number of detected repeats is greater than the number of tolerated repeats. The number of tolerated repeats is zero by default.

The following filter chain will eliminate all repeats:

```
<filter class="chapter6.RepeatFilter"/>
```

Running the chapter6.Sample1 application with the *examples/chapter6/repeat1.xml* configuration script, you shall notice that all repeat logs are removed. The script *repeat2.xml,* in the same folder, also removes repeat logs but only after the second occurrence.

For extra emphasis, allow me to repeat that in order to implement a custom filter it is sufficient to subclass the org.apache.log4j.spi.Filter class by implementing the decide(LoggingEvent) method and adding any setter/getter methods as appropriate for each filter option.

7

DIAGNOSTIC CONTEXTS

Lock the doors. —LEROY CAIN
Flight Director, Columbia Mission Control

One of the design goals of log4j is to audit and debug complex distributed applications. Most real-world distributed systems need to deal with multiple clients simultaneously. In a typical multithreaded implementation of such a system, different threads will handle different clients. A possible but discouraged approach to differentiate the logging output of one client from another consists of instantiating a new and separate logger for each client. This technique promotes the proliferation of loggers and considerably increases their management overhead. A lighter technique consists of uniquely stamping each log request servicing a given client. Neil Harrison described this method in the book "Patterns for Logging Diagnostic Messages," in Pattern Languages of Program Design 3, edited by R. Martin, D. Riehle, and F. Buschmann (Addison-Wesley, 1997). Log4j offers two variants of this technique: Mapped Diagnostic Contexts (MDC) and Nested Diagnostic Contexts (NDC).

Mapped Diagnostic Contexts

To uniquely stamp each request, the user puts contextual information into the MDC, the abbreviation of Mapped Diagnostic Context. The public interface of the MDC class is shown below.

```java
package org.apache.log4j;

public class MDC {
    // Put a context value (the o parameter) as identified by key into
    // the current thread's context map.
    static void put(String key, Object o);

    // Get the context identified by key.
    static Object get(String key);

    // Remove or clear the context identified by key.
    static void remove(String key)
}
```

The MDC class contains only static methods. It lets the developer to place information in a "diagnostic context" that can be subsequently retrieved by certain log4j components. *The MDC manages contextual information on a per thread basis.* Typically, while starting to service a new client request, the developer will insert pertinent contextual information, such as the client id, client's IP address, request parameters etc. into the MDC. Log4j components, if appropriately configured, will automatically include this information in each log entry. The next application named SimpleMDC demonstrates this basic principle.

Example 7-1: A very simple example of MDC usage (examples/chapter7/SimpleMDC.java)

```java
package chapter7;
import org.apache.log4j.Logger;
import org.apache.log4j.MDC;
import org.apache.log4j.ConsoleAppender;
import org.apache.log4j.PatternLayout;

public class SimpleMDC {

  static public void main(String[] args) throws Exception {
    // One can put values in the MDC at any time. We begin by
    // inserting the key "first" and its associated value
    MDC.put("first", "Dorothy");

    // Configure log4j
    PatternLayout layout=
                    new PatternLayout("%c %X{first} %X{last} %m%n");
    ConsoleAppender appender = new ConsoleAppender(layout);
    Logger root = Logger.getRootLogger();
    root.addAppender(appender);

    // get a logger
    Logger logger = Logger.getLogger(SimpleMDC1.class);

    // We now insert the key "last" and its associated value
    MDC.put("last", "Parker");

    // The most beautiful two words in the English language
    // according to Dorothy Parker:
    logger.info("Check enclosed.");
    logger.debug("The most beautiful two words in English.");

    MDC.put("first", "Richard");
    MDC.put("last", "Nixon");
    logger.info("I am not a crook.");
    logger.info("Attributed to the former US president. 17 Nov 1973.");
  }
}
```

The main method starts by associating the value "Dorothy" with the key "first" in the MDC. You can place as many value/key associations in the MDC as you wish.

Multiple insertions with the same key will overwrite older values. The code then proceeds to configure log4j. Note the usage of the %X specifier within the Pat- ternLayout conversion pattern. The %X conversion specifier is employed twice, once for the key "first" and once for the key "last". After configuring the root log- ger, the code associates the value "Parker" with the key "last". It then invokes the logger twice with different messages. The code finishes by setting the MDC to dif- ferent values and issuing several logging requests. Running SimpleMDC1 yields:

```
> java chapter7.SimpleMDC

Dorothy Parker - Check enclosed.
Dorothy Parker - The most beautiful two words in English.
Richard Nixon - I am not a crook.
Richard Nixon - Attributed to the former US president. 17 Nov 1973.
```

The SimpleMDC application illustrates how log4j layouts, if configured appropri- ately, automatically output MDC information. Moreover, the information placed into the MDC can be used by multiple logger invocations.

Mapped Diagnostic Contexts shine brightest within client server architectures. Typically, multiple clients will be served by multiple threads on the server. Al- though the methods in the MDC class are static, the diagnostic context is managed on a per thread basis, allowing each server thread to bear a distinct MDC stamp. MDC operations such as put() and get() affect the MDC of the *current* thread only. The MDC in other threads remain unaffected. Given that MDC information is managed on a per thread basis, each thread will have its own copy of the MDC. Thus, there is no need for the developer to worry about thread-safety or synchronization when pro- gramming with the MDC because it safely and transparently handles these issues.

The next example is somewhat more advanced. It shows how the MDC can be used in a client-server setting. The server-side implements the NumberCruncher inter- face shown in Example 7-2 below. The NumberCruncher interface contains a single method named factor(). Using RMI technology, client invokes the fac- tor() method of the server application to retrieve the distinct factors of an integer.

Example 7-2: The service interface (examples/chapter7/NumberCruncher .java)

```
package chapter7;
import java.rmi.Remote;
import java.rmi.RemoteException;

public interface NumberCruncher extends Remote {
  // Return the distinct factors of an integer
  int[] factor(int number) throws RemoteException;
}
```

The `NumberCruncherServer` application, listed in Example 7-3 below, implements the `NumberCruncher` interface. Its `main` method exports an RMI Registry on the local host that accepts requests on a well-known port.

Example 7-3: The server side (examples/chapter7/NumberCruncheServer.java)

```
package chapter7;

import java.rmi.*;
import java.util.Vector;

import org.apache.log4j.*;
import org.apache.log4j.xml.DOMConfigurator;

public class NumberCruncherServer extends UnicastRemoteObject
        implements NumberCruncher {

  static Logger logger = Logger.getLogger(NumberCruncherServer.class);

  public NumberCruncherServer() throws RemoteException {
  }

  public int[] factor(int number) throws RemoteException {

    // The client's host is an important source of information.
    try {
      MDC.put("client", this.getClientHost());
    } catch(java.rmi.server.ServerNotActiveException e) {
      logger.warn("Caught unexpected ServerNotActiveException.", e);
    }

    // The information contained within the request is another source
    // of distinctive information. It might reveal the users name,
    // date of request, request ID etc. In servlet type environments,
    // useful information is contained in the HttpRequest or in the
    // HttpSession.
    MDC.put("number", new Integer(number));

    logger.info("Beginning to factor.");
    if(number <= 0) {
      throw new IllegalArgumentException(number
                                    +" is not a positive integer.");
    } else if(number == 1) {
      return new int[] {1};
    }

    Vector factors = new Vector();
    int n = number;

    for(int i = 2; (i <= n) && (i*i <= number); i++) {
      // It is bad practice to place log statements within tight
      // loops. It is done here to show interleaved log output from
      // different requests.
```

```
      logger.debug("Trying to see if " + i + " is a factor.");

      if((n % i) == 0) {
       logger.info("Found factor "+i);
       factors.addElement(new Integer(i));
       do {
         n /= i;
       } while((n % i) == 0);
      }
      // Placing artificial delays in tight-loops will also lead to
      // sub-optimal results. :-)
      delay(100);
    }

    if(n != 1) {
      logger.info("Found factor "+n);
      factors.addElement(new Integer(n));
    }

    int len = factors.size();

    int[] result = new int[len];
    for(int i = 0; i < len; i++) {
      result[i] = ((Integer) factors.elementAt(i)).intValue();
    }

    // clean up
    MDC.remove("client");
    MDC.remove("number");

    return result;
  }

  static void usage(String msg) {
    System.err.println(msg);
    System.err.println(
      "Usage: java chapter7.NumberCruncherServer configFile\n"
     + "    where configFile is a log4j configuration file.");
    System.exit(1);
  }

  public static void delay(int millis) {
    try{Thread.currentThread().sleep(millis);}
    catch(InterruptedException e) {}
  }

  public static void main(String[] args) {
    if(args.length != 1)
      usage("Wrong number of arguments.");

    String configFile = args[0];
    if(configFile.endsWith(".xml")) {
      new DOMConfigurator().configure(configFile);
    } else {
```

```
      new PropertyConfigurator().configure(configFile);
    }

    NumberCruncherServer ncs;

    try {
      ncs = new NumberCruncherServer();
      logger.info("Creating registry.");
      Registry registry =
               LocateRegistry.createRegistry(Registry.REGISTRY_PORT);
      registry.rebind("Factor", ncs);
      logger.info("NumberCruncherServer bound and ready.");
    } catch(Exception e) {
      logger.error("Could not bind NumberCruncherServer.", e);
      return;
    }
  }
}
```

The implementation of the `factor(int number)` method is of particular relevance. It starts by putting the client's hostname into the MDC under the key "client". The number to factor, as requested by the client, is put into the MDC under the key "number". After computing the distinct factors of the integer parameter, the result is returned to the client. Before returning the result however, the values for the "client" and "number" are cleared by calling the MDC.`remove` method. Normally, an `put()` operation should be balanced by the corresponding `remove()` operation. Otherwise, the MDC will contain stale values for certain keys. I would recommend that whenever possible `remove()` operations be performed within `finally` blocks, ensuring their invocation regardless of the execution path of the code.

After these theoretical explanations, we are ready to run the number cruncher example. Start the server with the following command:

```
java chapter7.NumberCruncherServer chapter7/mdc1.properties
```

The configuration file *mdc1.properties* is listed below.

```
log4j.rootLogger=debug, CON
log4j.appender.CON=org.apache.log4j.ConsoleAppender
log4j.appender.CON.layout=org.apache.log4j.PatternLayout
log4j.appender.CON.layout.ConversionPattern=%-4r [%t] %-5p \
  C:%X{client} N:%X{number} - %m%n
```

Note the use of the %X conversion specifier within the **ConversionPattern** option.

The following command starts an instance of `NumberCruncherClient` application:

```
java chapter7.NumberCruncherClient hostname
```

where *hostname* is the host where the `NumberCruncherServer` is running.

Executing multiple instances of the client and requesting the server to factor the numbers 129 from the first client and shortly thereafter the number 71 from the second client, the server outputs the following (edited to fit):

```
0      [main] INFO  C: N: - Creating registry.
20     [main] INFO  C: N: - NumberCruncherServer bound and ready.
57213  [RMI Connection(11)] INFO  C:eitan N:129 - Beginning to factor.
57213  [RMI Connection(11)] DEBUG C:eitan N:129 - Trying 2 as a factor.
57313  [RMI Connection(11)] DEBUG C:eitan N:129 - Trying 3 as a factor.
57313  [RMI Connection(11)] INFO  C:eitan N:129 - Found factor 3
57413  [RMI Connection(11)] DEBUG C:eitan N:129 - Trying 4 as a factor.
57513  [RMI Connection(11)] DEBUG C:eitan N:129 - Trying 5 as a factor.
57613  [RMI Connection(11)] DEBUG C:eitan N:129 - Trying 6 as a factor.
57703  [RMI Connection(12)] INFO  C:eitan N:71 - Beginning to factor.
57703  [RMI Connection(12)] DEBUG C:eitan N:71 - Trying 2 as a factor.
57713  [RMI Connection(11)] DEBUG C:eitan N:129 - Trying 7 as a factor.
57803  [RMI Connection(12)] DEBUG C:eitan N:71 - Trying 3 as a factor.
57813  [RMI Connection(11)] DEBUG C:eitan N:129 - Trying 8 as a factor.
57904  [RMI Connection(12)] DEBUG C:eitan N:71 - Trying 4 as a factor.
57914  [RMI Connection(11)] DEBUG C:eitan N:129 - Trying 9 as a factor.
58004  [RMI Connection(12)] DEBUG C:eitan N:71 - Trying 5 as a factor.
58014  [RMI Connection(11)] DEBUG C:eitan N:129 - Trying 10 as a factor.
58104  [RMI Connection(12)] DEBUG C:eitan N:71 - Trying 6 as a factor.
58114  [RMI Connection(11)] DEBUG C:eitan N:129 - Trying 11a factor.
58204  [RMI Connection(12)] DEBUG C:eitan N:71 - Trying 7 as a factor.
58214  [RMI Connection(11)] INFO  C:eitan N:129 - Found factor 43
58304  [RMI Connection(12)] DEBUG C:eitan N:71 - Trying 8 as a factor.
58404  [RMI Connection(12)] INFO  C:eitan N:71 - Found factor 71
```

The clients were run from a machine called "eitan" as can be seen in the above output. Even if the server processes the requests of clients near-simultaneously in separate threads, the logging output pertaining to each client request can be distinguished by studying the output of the MDC. Note for example the stamp associated with "number", i.e. the number to factor.

The attentive reader might have observed that the thread name could also have been used to distinguish each request. The thread name can cause confusion if the server side technology recycles threads. In that case, it may be hard to determine the boundaries of each request, that is, when a given thread finishes servicing a request and when it begins servicing the next. Because the MDC is under the control of the application developer, MDC stamps do no suffer from this problem.

The MDC class requires JDK 1.2 or above. Under JDK 1.1 the MDC will always return empty values but otherwise will not affect or harm your application.

Nested Diagnostic Contexts

The NDC, the abbreviation of Nested Diagnostic Context, closely resembles the MDC. The NDC also manages information on a per thread basis but as a stack, not a map. The salient methods of the NDC class are listed below.

```
public class NDC {

    // Add diagnostic context for the current thread.
    public static void push(String message);

    // Remove the top of the context from the NDC.
    public static String pop();

    // Remove the diagnostic context for this thread.
    public static void remove();
}
```

The NDC is managed per thread as a stack of contextual information. Note that all methods of the org.apache.log4j.NDC class are static. Assuming that NDC printing is turned on, every time a log request is made, the appropriate log4j component will include the entire NDC stack for the current thread in the log output. This is done without the intervention of the user, who is responsible only for placing the correct information in the NDC by using the push() and pop() methods at a few well-defined points in the code.

Given that NDC information is managed on a per thread basis, each thread will have its own copy of the NDC. Operations such as push and pop affect the NDC of the *current* thread only. The NDC of other threads remain unaffected. Thus, there is no need for the developer to worry about thread-safety or synchronization issues when programming with the NDC. It safely handles these issues transparently.

We now list an NDC version of Example 7-1 that we studied earlier.

Example 7-4: A very simple example of NDC usage (examples/chapter7/SimpleNDC.java)

```
package chapter7;

import org.apache.log4j.Logger;
import org.apache.log4j.NDC;
import org.apache.log4j.ConsoleAppender;
import org.apache.log4j.PatternLayout;

public class SimpleNDC {

    static public void main(String[] args) throws Exception {

        // Configure log4j, note the %x conversion specifier.
```

```
PatternLayout layout = new PatternLayout("%x - %m%n");
ConsoleAppender appender = new ConsoleAppender(layout);
Logger root = Logger.getRootLogger();
root.addAppender(appender);

// get a logger
Logger logger = Logger.getLogger(SimpleNDC.class);

NDC.push("Dorothy");
NDC.push("Parker");
logger.info("Check enclosed.");
logger.info("The most beautiful two words in English.");
NDC.pop();
NDC.pop(); // we need to pop twice because we pushed twice.

NDC.push("Richard Nixon");
logger.info("I am not a crook.");
logger.info("Attributed to the former US president. 17 Nov 1973.");
NDC.pop(); // pop once, because we pushed only once.

NDC.remove();
  }
}
```

Executing the `chapter7.SimpleNDC` application will yield the following output.

```
Dorothy Parker - Check enclosed.
Dorothy Parker - The most beautiful two words in English.
Richard Nixon - I am not a crook.
Richard Nixon - Attributed to the former US president. 17 Nov 1973.
```

Note that the %x conversion specifier in `PatternLayout` displays the full contents of the NDC, not just the top value. Moreover, NDC push operations must be balanced by an equal number of `pop` operations. Otherwise, the NDC will contain inaccurate information. I would recommend that whenever possible `pop()` operations be performed within `finally` blocks. This ensures that pops are performed correctly regardless of the execution path of your code.

Heavy duty systems should call the `remove()` method when leaving the `run()` method of a thread. This ensures that the memory used by the thread can be freed by the Java garbage collector. Each thread that created a diagnostic context by calling `NDC.push()` should call this method before exiting. Otherwise, the memory used by the *entire* thread[24] cannot be reclaimed by the VM garbage collector. Thus, if your application creates and destroys threads dynamically, your application will soon run out of memory. As this is such an important problem in heavy duty sys-

---

[24] Each and every Java thread consumes approximately 4MB of memory.

tems and because it is difficult to always guarantee that the `remove` method is called before exiting a thread, this method has been augmented to lazily remove references to dead threads. In practice, this means that you can be a little sloppy and occasionally forget to call `remove()` before exiting a thread. However, you must call the `remove()` method once in a while. If you never call it, then your application will eventually run out of memory.

Contrary to the MDC which requires JDK 1.2, the NDC class remains compatible with JDK 1.1 or above. Given that the next version of log4j, namely version 1.3, will be based on JDK 1.2, the `NDC.remove()` method will become obsolete.

8

EXTENDING LOG4J

It is not knowledge, but the act of learning, not possession but the act of getting there, which grants the greatest enjoyment. When I have clarified and exhausted a subject, then I turn away from it, in order to go into darkness again; the never-satisfied man is so strange if he has completed a structure, then it is not in order to dwell in it peacefully, but in order to begin another. I imagine the world conqueror must feel thus, who, after one kingdom is scarcely conquered, stretches out his arms for others.

—KARL FRIEDRICH GAUSS, Letter to Bolyai, 1808.

Style, like sheer silk, too often hides eczema.

—ALBERT CAMUS, *The Fall*

The imaginative power of an unstructured community well exceeds that of the dedicated but few. Recognizing this fact and as an open source project log4j strives[25] to be as extensible as possible in order to unleash the creative minds of its community. Earlier chapters have touched the topic of custom appenders, custom layouts and custom filters. Custom appenders, layouts and layouts merely leverage log4j's modular design. However, many users frequently express their desire to extend the core classes in log4j. Other concerns such as overall reliability and backward compatibility often enter in violent conflict with demands for extensibility. The tug-of-war between the forces of change and the forces of stability can be observed in other frameworks as well. This chapter presents ways of extending core log4j classes. It will also mention the caveats of each extension.

---

[25] I say "strives" because engineering a truly extensible framework takes considerably more effort than producing an otherwise useful library.

Writing your own Levels

The set of pre-built levels in log4j, that is OFF, FATAL, ERROR, WARN, INFO, DE-
BUG, ALL is purposefully small. Conjugated with the logger hierarchy, the limited
set of levels offers considerable flexibility in categorizing log statements. A larger
set often ends up confusing developers instead doing any good. Take for example
the set of levels defined in the venerable Syslog logging utility found in Unix oper-
ating systems. The Syslog levels are listed below.

```
#define EMERG     0   /* system is unusable                   */
#define ALERT     1   /* action must be taken immediately */
#define CRIT      2   /* critical conditions               */
#define ERR       3   /* error conditions                  */
#define WARNING   4   /* warning conditions                */
#define NOTICE    5   /* normal but significant condition */
#define INFO      6   /* informational                     */
#define DEBUG     7   /* debug-level messages              */
```

I personally find it hard to distinguish between the NOTICE and INFO levels or
between the EMERG, ALERT and CRIT levels. While it may be justified to define
new levels under certain circumstances, a larger set of levels is not necessarily better.

In log4j, each level has a string representation which matches the name of the level.
For example, the level INFO has string representation "INFO". Most importantly
however, levels are ordered according to their severity. For example, the level
WARN holds a higher severity than INFO. When adding a new level, the foremost
question you must ask yourself is how the severity of the new level compares to
those of existing levels. If the question cannot be answered easily, then you should
probably dismiss the new level.

Log4j users frequently advocate the addition of a new level, namely the TRACE
level, possessing a lower severity than the existing DEBUG level. These users claim
that the TRACE level would allow developers to categorize less important debugging messages. Given that the constructor in the Level class is protected, new levels can only be added by sub-classing the Level class. The XLevel class listed
below extends Level, hence its name. Its purpose is to add a new level called
TRACE.

Example 8-1: Adding the TRACE level (examples/chapter8/XLevel .java)

```java
package chapter8;
import org.apache.log4j.Level;

/**
 * The XLevel class extends the Level class by introducing a new
 * level called TRACE. TRACE has a lower level than DEBUG. */
public class final XLevel extends Level {

  static public final int  TRACE_INT   = Level.DEBUG_INT - 1;
  private static String TRACE_STR  = "TRACE";
  public static final XLevel TRACE = new XLevel(TRACE_INT,
                                            TRACE_STR, 7);

  protected XLevel(int level, String strLevel, int syslogEquiv) {
    super(level, strLevel, syslogEquiv);
  }

  /**
   * Convert the String argument to a level. If the conversion
   * fails then this method returns {@link #TRACE}. */
  public static Level toLevel(String sArg) {
    return (Level) toLevel(sArg, XLevel.TRACE);
  }

  /**
   * Convert the String argument to a level. If the
   * conversion fails, return the level specified by the
   * second argument, i.e. defaultValue. */
  public static Level toLevel(String sArg, Level defaultValue) {
    if(sArg == null) {
      return defaultValue;
    }
    String stringVal = sArg.toUpperCase();

    if(stringVal.equals(TRACE_STR)) {
      return XLevel.TRACE;
    }
    return Level.toLevel(sArg, defaultValue);
  }

  /**
   * Convert an integer passed as argument to a level. If the
   * conversion fails, then this method returns {@link #DEBUG}.
   * */
  public static Level toLevel(int i)
                              throws  IllegalArgumentException {
```

```
      if(i == TRACE_INT) {
        return XLevel.TRACE;
      } else {
        return Level.toLevel(i);
      }
   }
}
```

The XLevel class begins by defining the integer and string representation for the
TRACE level. The integer field TRACE_INT takes a value just under that of DE-
BUG_INT. The field named TRACE (of type XLevel) holds our newly defined
level. It is marked as public, final and static. Given that the constructor of the
XLevel class is protected, it can only be called within the XLevel class or from
within sub-classes of XLevel.

After instantiating the TRACE field, the XLevel class proceeds to implement three
conversion methods all named toLevel(), but featuring different signatures.
These methods convert incoming integer or string parameters and return the corresponding Level instance. These methods directly handle the TRACE case and delegate the conversion work for the remaining cases to the appropriate conversion
method of the parent class.

You can pass the XLevel.TRACE object wherever an object of type Level is expected. In particular, the Logger.log methods are specifically designed to deal
with custom levels. In configuration files, a custom level value can be specified in
the form "level#classname" which translates to "trace#chapter8.XLevel" in this
example. The next exercise demonstrates the use of our new custom level.

Example 8-2: Using the TRACE level (examples/chapter8/UsingTrace .java)

```
package chapter8;
import chapter8.XLevel;
import org.apache.log4j.Logger;
import org.apache.log4j.PropertyConfigurator;
import org.apache.log4j.xml.DOMConfigurator;

public class UsingTrace {
  final static Logger logger = Logger.getLogger(UsingTrace.class);

  public static void main(String[] args) {
    if(args.length != 1) {
      System.err.println("Usage: java chapter8.UsingTrace "
                         + "configFile");
      System.exit(1);
    }
    String configFile = args[0];
```

```
      if(configFile.endsWith(".xml")) {
        new DOMConfigurator().configure(configFile);
      } else {
        new PropertyConfigurator().configure(configFile);
      }
      logger.debug("Now there are fields where Troy once was.");
      logger.log(XLevel.TRACE, "Thus, Troy has left no tangible
                          + " trace.");
  }
}
```

Invoking the *UsingTrace* application with the configuration file *examples/chapter8/trace1.properties* will yield the following output:

```
DEBUG - Now there are fields where Troy once was.
TRACE - Thus, Troy has left no tangible trace.
```

The configuration file *examples/chapter8/trace1.properties* is listed next.

```
log4j.rootLogger=TRACE#chapter8.XLevel, CON
log4j.appender.CON=org.apache.log4j.ConsoleAppender
log4j.appender.CON.layout=org.apache.log4j.PatternLayout
log4j.appender.CON.layout.ConversionPattern=%-5p - %m%n
```

Its XML equivalent is:

```
<?xml version="1.0" encoding="UTF-8" ?>
<!DOCTYPE log4j:configuration SYSTEM "log4j.dtd">

<log4j:configuration

xmlns:log4j='http://jakarta.apache.org/log4j/'>

  <appender name="STDOUT"
            class="org.apache.log4j.ConsoleAppender">
    <layout class="org.apache.log4j.PatternLayout">
      <param name="ConversionPattern" value="%-5p - %m%n"/>
    </layout>
  </appender>
  <root>
    <level value="trace#chapter8.XLevel"/>
    <appender-ref ref="STDOUT"/>
  </root>
</log4j:configuration>
```

The level element can also be written as:

```
<level value="trace" class="chapter8.XLevel"/>
```

Had we not set the root level to TRACE but left at its default value, i.e. DEBUG, then the trace statement would not have appeared on the console.

Once defined, log4j treats custom levels the same way as the built-in levels. Custom levels can appear in configuration files. They can be passed as arguments to custom filters or serialized across the wire. Given that Java is a strongly typed language, log4j cannot transparently add printing methods associated with the new level. In other words, the trace() method does not magically appear in the Logger class. One must use the generic log() method instead. This limitation can be circumvented by either extending the Logger class or by wrapping the Logger class. Each approach has its own advantages as well as disadvantages.

Writing your own Logger class

Object oriented languages offer built-in means for extending functionality of any class by *derivation* or *sub-classing*. Most developers are drawn to programming because of their curiosity and their innate inclination to tinkering. Shortly after getting familiar with log4j, many developers start imagining new ways for extending log4j functionality. Given that the Logger class plays a central role within the log4j framework, extending the Logger class appears as the most obvious approach to implementing any new desired core functionality. Although natural, subclassing the Logger class conceals a severe pitfall as we shall now illustrate.

Assume MyLogger class extends Logger by adding a new method called foo(). Given that the foo() method is only available to MyLogger objects, code wishing to invoke the foo() method must make sure to get a reference to a MyLogger object. Let us also assume the existence of a factory method, say getMyLogger, in the MyLogger class. The return type of this factory method can be Logger or MyLogger. Suppose the returned type is MyLogger. In that case, the typical usage pattern would be:

```
MyLogger ml = MyLogger.getMyLogger("x.y.z");
ml.foo(....);
```

Now assume some code instantiates the "x.y.z" logger before MyLogger.getMyLogger is called. As in,

```
Logger l = Logger.getLogger("x.y.z");
MyLogger ml = MyLogger.getMyLogger("x.y.z");
```

Unless MyLogger objects live detached and independent lives form log4j's named hierarchy, the second line of code cannot possibly succeed because the "x.y.z" logger is already created. It is necessarily of type Logger. Remember that when asked to manufacture a logger of a certain name, log4j will return a reference to any existing logger of that name. This functionality is at the core of log4j. It cannot be modified without tearing apart the hierarchical arrangement of loggers.

The problem does not get any more tractable had we assumed that the return type of `getMyLogger` was `Logger`. The following code would systematically throw a `ClassCastException`.

```
Logger l = Logger.getLogger("bad");
MyLogger ml = (MyLogger) MyLogger.getLogger("bad"); // causes CCE
```

The problem occurs because the invocation of the `getMyLogger` method will retrieve the `Logger` created by earlier `getLogger` invocation. This instance is a `Logger` object and cannot be cast as `MyLogger`.

To avoid the paralyzing damage caused by class cast exceptions, earlier versions of log4j introduced configuration directives instructing configurators to set the logger factory which forced the production of loggers of the desired type. This solution works as long as the application developer controls the java code as well as the log4j configuration files. Unfortunately, many developers do not enjoy this luxury. As we have seen in Chapter 3, the configuration of log4j is the responsibility of the end-user or more generally the application deployer. Experience, often bitter, has revealed that permitting configuration files to set the logger factory was an unsafe practice. Consequently, this manual shies away from providing the syntax for specifying the logger factory in configuration files. We will introduce a safer and more powerful, albeit more complicated sub-classing architecture later in this chapter.

The crucial point to retain from the above discussion is that modifying the interface of the `Logger` class through sub-classing is inherently unsafe. I strongly discourage developers from sub-classing the `Logger` class in order to modify its interface. However, sub-classing can be used to modify the *behavior* of existing `Logger` methods as long as no methods are added or removed, nor their signatures modified.

However, the interface of the `Logger` class can be safely modified by encapsulation a.k.a. wrapping.

Wrapping the Logger class

The decorator or wrapper design pattern provides a common alternative to subclassing in order to attach new responsibilities to objects. The oft-cited "Design Pattern" book by Eric Gamma et al. formally describes the wrapper pattern. Wrappers can be used to add responsibilities to individual objects dynamically and transparently, or on the contrary, to withdraw responsibilities. Wrappers can save the day when extension by sub-classing is impractical, which happens to be the case for the `Logger` class.

The wrapper encloses the component to be extended. Wrapper must also conform to match the interface of the wrapped object such that wrapper objects can be transparently interchanged with the original object. However, since the `Logger` is a class and not an interface, and because it cannot be easily sub-classed, `Logger` wrappers can not act as a transparent enclosure. This hardly appears to be a serious issue because `Logger` objects rarely act as data types or subjects of transformations. One usually invokes logger objects, not act on them. Thus, I will continue to use the term wrapper even if it does not match the formal definition of the wrapper design pattern.

A `Logger` wrapper can serve many purposes. For example, it can

- add new methods to handle custom levels

- remove seldom used methods which clutter the `Logger` class

- automatically handle nested exceptions

- add internationalization features beyond those already supported in the `Logger` class

- add new methods to handle resource bundles

These are just a few reasons for extending the `Logger` class. One could imagine many other valid ones.

Developers have not waited for the appearance of this manual to write wrappers. I frequently receive email where a user runs into a problem with their wrapper and requests help. More often than not, these wrappers contain errors such that the cost of inactive (or disabled) logging statements is multiplied by a factor of 1'000 (one thousand) compared to direct log4j usage. The most common error in wrapper classes is the invocation of the `Logger.getLogger()` method for each log request. Repeatedly retrieving loggers is guaranteed to wreak havoc on your application's performance. *Really*!

For didactical purposes, let us write a wrapper class that adds support for the `TRACE` custom level we created earlier. Let `MyLogger` be the name of this wrapper. To spice up the exercise, `MyLogger` will also automatically print nested exceptions.

Example 8-3: Our first wrapper (examples/chapter/MyLogger.java)

```
package chapter8;

import chapter8.XLevel;
import org.apache.log4j.Logger;
import org.apache.log4j.Level;
import org.apache.log4j.PropertyConfigurator;
import org.apache.log4j.xml.DOMConfigurator;
import java.lang.reflect.Method;

public class MyLogger {
  // Our fully qualified class name.
  static String FQCN = MyLogger.class.getName();
  static boolean JDK14 = false;

  static {
    String version =  System.getProperty("java.version");
    if(version != null) {
      JDK14 = version.startsWith("1.4");
    }
  }

  private Logger logger;

  public MyLogger(String name) {
    this.logger = Logger.getLogger(name);
  }

  public MyLogger(Class clazz) {
    this(clazz.getName());
  }

  public void trace(Object msg) {
    logger.log(FQCN, XLevel.TRACE, msg, null);
  }
  public void trace(Object msg, Throwable t) {
    logger.log(FQCN, XLevel.TRACE, msg, t);
    logNestedException(XLevel.TRACE, msg, t);
  }
  public boolean isTraceEnabled() {
    return logger.isEnabledFor(XLevel.TRACE);
  }

  public void debug(Object msg) {
    logger.log(FQCN, Level.DEBUG, msg, null);
  }
```

```
public void debug(Object msg, Throwable t) {
  logger.log(FQCN, Level.DEBUG, msg, t);
  logNestedException(Level.DEBUG, msg, t);
}
public boolean isDebugEnabled() {
  return logger.isDebugEnabled();
}

public void info(Object msg) {
  logger.log(FQCN, Level.INFO, msg, null);
}
public void info(Object msg, Throwable t) {
  logger.log(FQCN, Level.INFO, msg, t);
  logNestedException(Level.INFO, msg, t);
}
public boolean isInfoEnabled() {
  return logger.isInfoEnabled();
}

public void warn(Object msg) {
  logger.log(FQCN, Level.WARN, msg, null);
}
public void warn(Object msg, Throwable t) {
  logger.log(FQCN, Level.WARN, msg, t);
  logNestedException(Level.WARN, msg, t);
}

public void error(Object msg) {
  logger.log(FQCN, Level.ERROR, msg, null);
}
public void error(Object msg, Throwable t) {
  logger.log(FQCN, Level.ERROR, msg, t);
  logNestedException(Level.ERROR, msg, t);
}

public void fatal(Object msg) {
  logger.log(FQCN, Level.FATAL, msg, null);
}
public void fatal(Object msg, Throwable t) {
  logger.log(FQCN, Level.FATAL, msg, t);
  logNestedException(Level.FATAL, msg, t);
}
void logNestedException(Level level, Object msg, Throwable t) {
 if(t == null)
    return;

  try {
    Class tC = t.getClass();
    Method mA[] = tC.getMethods();
```

```
      Method nextThrowableMethod = null;
      for(int i=0; i < mA.length ; i++) {
        if(("getCause".equals(mA[i].getName()) && !JDK14)
            || "getRootCause".equals(mA[i].getName())
            || "getNextException".equals( mA[i].getName())
            || "getException".equals( mA[i].getName())) {
          // check param types
          Class params[] = mA[i].getParameterTypes();
          if(params==null || params.length==0) {
            // just found the getter for the nested throwable
            nextThrowableMethod=mA[i];
            break; // no need to search further
          }
        }
      }
      if(nextThrowableMethod != null) {
        // get the nested throwable and log it
        Throwable next =
        (Throwable)nextThrowableMethod.invoke(t, new Object[0]);
        if(nextT != null) {
          this.logger.log(FQCN, level,
                          "Previous log CONTINUED", nextT);
        }
      }
    } catch(Exception e) {
      // do nothing
    }
  }
}
```

There are several noteworthy points about `MyLogger`. For starters, it does not derive from `Logger`. Instead, each instance of `MyLogger` encapsulates a logger instance. The encapsulated logger instance is marked as private final. The logger
field is assigned within the `MyLogger` constructors. Here are the relevant lines
from *MyLogger.java*.

```
private final Logger logger;

public MyLogger(String name) {
  this.logger = Logger.getLogger(name);
}
public MyLogger(Class clazz) {
  this(clazz.getName());
}
```

The reference to the enclosed logger object is obtained by invoking the `Log-`
`ger.getLogger` method. However, this is done only once within the lifetime of a

MyLogger object. Assuming most MyLogger variables are class static, MyLogger constructor will not be called frequently enough to degrade performance.

The mysterious FCQN variable, declared at the start of MyLogger class, helps log4j to obtain the correct localization information, as output by the %F, %C, %L, %F conversion specifiers in PatternLayout. Without it, log4j will be tricked into thinking that MyLogger is the caller instead of the class which really invoked a MyLogger instance. The printing methods in MyLogger class simply forward the work to the enclosed logger object. Here is how the debug method does it.

```
public void debug(Object msg) {
   logger.log(FQCN, Level.DEBUG, msg, null);
}
```

The debug method does not call its namesake in the Logger class. It calls the generic Logger.log() method which accepts the FCQN variable as a parameter. The case of the trace method is fairly similar. It passes the custom level XLevel.TRACE as a level parameter; otherwise, it is no different from the other printing methods in MyLogger.

```
public void trace(Object msg) {
   logger.log(FQCN, XLevel.TRACE, msg, null);
}
```

For each of the printing methods in the Logger class there is a variant that takes a throwable as a second parameter. MyLogger offers the same variants but these behave somewhat differently. If the throwable parameter contains a nested exception, it will be automatically printed in a separate logging statement by calling the logNestedException method. As in,

```
public void error(Object msg, Throwable t) {
   logger.log(FQCN, Level.ERROR, msg, t);
   logNestedException(Level.ERROR, msg, t);
}
```

Nested exceptions are discovered by studying the class of the throwable object by reflection. When a nested exception is available, then the logNestedException method invokes the generic log method of the encapsulated logger, with the nested exception passed as the last parameter. The nested exception returned by the get-Cause method, if it exists, is ignored under JDK 1.4 because this version of the JDK has built-in support for nested exceptions.

Our wrapper can be used almost the same way as the original Logger class as illustrated by the *UsingMyLogger* application.

Example 8-4: Using our wrapper (examples/chapter8/UsingMyLogger.java)

```
package chapter8;

import chapter8.XLevel;
import org.apache.log4j.Logger;
import org.apache.log4j.PropertyConfigurator;
import org.apache.log4j.xml.DOMConfigurator;

public class UsingMyLogger {
  final static MyLogger logger =
                            new MyLogger(UsingMyLogger.class);

  public static void main(String[] args) {
    if(args.length != 1) {
      System.err.println("Usage: java chapter8.UsingMyLogger "
                          + " configFile");
      System.exit(1);
    }
    String configFile = args[0];
    if(configFile.endsWith(".xml")) {
      new DOMConfigurator().configure(configFile);
    } else {
      new PropertyConfigurator().configure(configFile);
    }

    logger.trace("Hello from a MyLogger.");
    logger.warn("Here is a nested exception.)",
            new NestedException(new Exception("Root cause")));
  }
}
```

The code of the NestedException class is trivial. It is listed below for completeness.

```
class NestedException extends Exception {
  private Throwable cause;

  NestedException(Exception cause) {
    super();
    this.cause = cause;
  }
  public Throwable getCause() {
    return cause;
  }
}
```

Running *UsingMyLogger* application with the following configuration file:

Example 8-5: Configuration with caller information (examples/chapter8/myLogger1.properties)

```
log4j.rootLogger=TRACE#chapter8.XLevel, CON
log4j.appender.CON=org.apache.log4j.ConsoleAppender
log4j.appender.CON.layout=org.apache.log4j.PatternLayout
log4j.appender.CON.layout.ConversionPattern=%-5p (%C:%L) - %m%n
```

will result in the following output:

```
TRACE (chapter8.UsingMyLogger:24) - Hello from a MyLogger.
WARN  (chapter8.UsingMyLogger:25) - Here is a nested exception.
chapter8.NestedException
        at chapter8.UsingMyLogger.main(UsingMyLogger.java:25)
WARN  (chapter8.UsingMyLogger:25) - Previous log CONTINUED:
java.lang.Exception: Root cause
        at chapter8.UsingMyLogger.main(UsingMyLogger.java:25)
```

Comments on the Jakarta commons-logging package

Given that log4j is such a low-level library, most organizations are hesitant to tie their code to log4j, especially considering the new logging API included in JDK 1.4.

Before going forward, it is appropriate to mention that these two APIs are very similar. The classical usage pattern for log4j is:

```
import org.apache.log4j.Logger;

public class MyClass {
  final static Logger logger = Logger.getLogger("some.name");

  public void foo1() {
    logger.debug("Hello world.");
  }

  public void foo2() {
    logger.info("Another message.");
    logger.error("Stop that!",
                  new Exception("The earth is getting warmer."));
  }
}
```

As you are well aware by now, one of the important benefits of log4j is that it can be configured at run time using configuration scripts. You can have hundreds or

thousands of log statement but only one or two lines of Java code to configure
log4j.

The usage pattern for the JDK 1.4 logging API is:

```
import java.util.logging.Logger;

public class MyClass {
   final static Logger logger = Logger.getLogger("test");

   public void foo1() {
     logger.debug("Hello world.");
   }

   public void foo2() {
     logger.info("Another message.");
     logger.error("Stop that!",
                 new Exception("The earth is getting warmer."));
   }
}
```

Although the log4j API is at least two years older than JDK 1.4, notice the extent to
which the two APIs are similar. The JDK 1.4 logging API also supports configuration scripts. Being part of the JDK, some users reckon that the JSR47 API will sup-
plant log4j some time in the near future. Surprisingly enough, it is not easy to write
a complete logging API. Users come to realize they need the features present in
log4j but absent in JDK 1.4 logging. Moreover, log4j runs under JDK 1.1 or later
whereas JDK 1.4 logging requires, well, JDK 1.4. Most users can't afford to tie
their code to JDK 1.4. But they need logging and they need it now. A common
strategy for protecting against future changes and at the same time to benefit from
existing log4j features is to wrap log4j with a custom logging API.

The commons-logging API has gained popularity because it wraps multiple logging frameworks and postpones the choice of the underlying logging API to the
latest possible moment, that is to runtime. It is available at *http://jakar-
ta.apache.org/commons/logging.html.*

In order to support multiple logging frameworks transparently, the commons-
logging API has its own "discovery process" which depends on the resources
available to a particular class loader. In addition, the commons-logging API will
create its own logger wrapper for each and every class loader in use within your
application. The class loader based automatic discovery process is the principal
weakness of the commons-logging API due to its considerable complexity. Dealing
with class loader related problems requires that the developer understands class
loaders, as well as the class loader hierarchy of her particular J2EE container.

The problem's severity is not due to lazy users who do not bother to read the documentation. According to the java language, two classes loaded by different class loaders are *totally* incompatible even if they are bit-wise identical. If you opt for the commons-logging API, then the behavior of your system will depend on external circumstances which you, as a developer, cannot control. In general, all solutions based on class loading hacks are brittle and result in painful bugs. Moreover, these bugs can only be fixed by displacing jar files more or less at random. The real bug hides in the discovery process of commons-logging. It cannot be fixed without removing of the class loader dependency in the discovery process.

Unexpected interactions between log4j and a commons-logging wrapper API are also quite probable. The developers of the wrapper will suspect a log4j problem and conversely the log4j developers will suspect a wrapper problem. By increasing the number of components required for logging, the probability of bugs increases while the difficulty of resolving them increases by a higher factor. The justification for the existence of logging in the first place is to facilitate problem identification. As such, the logging component must be robust and simple to set up. The more complex the logging component gets, the less useful it becomes.

Since the primary goal of the commons-logging API is to discover and use the logging framework that is available at runtime, it can only cater for lowest common denominator of the different logging frameworks. As JDK 1.4 logging does not offer the same set of features as log4j, by using the common-logging API you would be missing those extra features, such as logging domains[26], Nested Diagnostic Contexts (NDC) and Mapped Diagnostic Contexts (MDC) which are essential features in server-type applications.

If for whatever reason you decide to drop log4j in favor of JDK 1.4 (or the other way around) a simple string search-and-replace operation will do. Most IDEs support search-and-replace operations on multiple files. Given the above, one should think twice before rushing to adopt the commons-logging API. I should emphasize that the commons-logging API is quite log4j friendly. For example, the current implementation will first search for log4j by default. The commons-logging API has probably facilitated the adoption of log4j by many users, especially through Tomcat and Struts. All the more, I remain quite worried about the unflattering user experience.

---

[26] Domains are a very useful feature planned for log4j version 1.3.

The wider context

The intended audience of this section is the authors of application servers, servlet containers and authors of general-purpose libraries.

Log4j is a low level API used in a variety of projects. Consequently, it is hard to make a priori assumptions about the environment where log4j will run. The problem is particularly acute in embedded components (e.g. libraries) that rely on log4j for their logging. The author of embedded component can rarely afford to make restrictive assumptions about the surrounding environment, a fortiori assumptions about logging.

The "logging separation" problem

Since time immemorial users have struggled to control the logging configuration of multiple web-applications deployed on the same servlet container (e.g. Tomcat). What does separation of logging mean? In a separated logging environment, each web-application can configure log4j in different ways such that the configuration of one web-application cannot interfere with the logging configuration of another web-application. A variant of this problem is the separation of web-application logging and logging by the servlet container itself. The problem extends by analogy to EJB containers.

When we talk about logging separation the following cases must be taken into consideration:

- Servlet classes that are used in a single web-application (unshared servlets). More generally, libraries or classes that are used by one and only one web-application (unshared libraries).

- Servlet classes that are used in a multiple web-applications (shared servlets). More generally, libraries or classes that are shared between multiple web-applications (shared libraries).

- Loggers which are class static variables.

- Loggers which are instance variables of the containing class.

- Loggers which are local variables of the containing class method.

In case logging separation cannot be achieved for a particular case, this must be well documented such that users become aware of potential problems and possibly avoid troublesome cases altogether. Let us study a number of possible solutions that address the "logging separation" problem.

First Solution

Assuming each web-application is loaded by a distinct class loader, then placing a copy of *log4j.jar* under *WEB-INF/lib/* directory of each web-application will automatically result in distinct log4j-logging universes. Simply put, each web-application will load its own distinct copy of log4j classes into memory. All such copies are invisible and inaccessible to each other.

This solution is not too complicated to set up but has drawbacks:

- Multiple copies of *log4j.jar* take more disk and memory space. On today's computers with huge disk spaces and memory, the waste of a few hundred kilobytes is hardly a serious issue.

- The Java class loader delegation model gives precedence to parent class loaders. This means that if *log4j.jar* is available on the CLASSPATH, or under *JAVA_HOME/jar/lib/ext* or to any class loader which is a parent of the web-application's class loader, then that copy of log4j will be loaded into memory and shared by all web-applications.

  The class loader approach is brittle: its success depends on external factors. If your environment is not setup properly then the solution won't work. If the container itself uses log4j and makes it visible to web-applications, it won't work. In general, solutions depending on class loader tricks don't very work well. They are complicated and fragile. Most Java developers, even experienced ones, do not understand class loaders. Dealing with class loader related problems requires that the developer understands class loaders as well as the class loader hierarchy of the particular container she is using. Different containers exhibit different class loading behaviors. In some cases, different versions of the *same* container behave differently.

- Assuming you are lucky and you successfully setup different log4j-logging environment for each web-application, then since every copy of the log4j classes are invisible to each other, they will also be invisible to any management entity. In other words, it will be impossible to manage the different log4j instances from a single management console.

Second solution

Log4j allows different applications live in their own parallel universe by using a
different LoggerRepository for each application. The main methods in the LoggerRepository interface are listed below.

```
package org.apache.log4j.spi;

public interface LoggerRepository {
  // Returns an enumeration of the currently existing loggers
  Enumeration getCurrentLoggers();

  // Create a new logger with the given name
  Logger getLogger(String name);

  // Create a new logger with the given name, delegate actual
  // creation to a LoggerFactory.
  Logger getLogger(String name, LoggerFactory factory)

  // Get the root logger
  Logger getRootLogger();

  // Get the repository-wide threshold
  Level getThreshold()

  // Is the respository disabled for a given level?
  boolean isDisabled(int level)

  // Reset the configuration of existing loggers. This does
  // not remove them.
  void resetConfiguration();

  // Set the repository-wide threshold.
  void setThreshold(Level level)
}
```

The Hierarchy class implements the LoggerRepository interface which arranges loggers in a tree according to their name. Log4j delegates the creation of
loggers to a default Hierarchy object. However, developers are free to maintain
and use their own hierarchy. Given that each hierarchy (i.e. logger repository)
manages its own separate logger tree, logging separation is a direct consequence of
this approach.

The Java Servlet API mandates a unique ServletContext for each web-
application. Thus, a web-application can set an attribute for a servlet context which
can be shared by all servlets and jsp pages of a web-application but remain invisi-

ble to other web-applications. In particular, an initialization servlet can create, set and configure an independent logger hierarchy in the servlet context. Subsequently, other servlets can obtain the hierarchy stored in the servlet context in order to retrieve logger instances. These logger instances will be attached to the particular hierarchy specific to the web-application.

Under the *examples/chapter8/multipleHiearchies/* directory you shall find two web-applications, namely *Hello* and *Tata*, that employ the technique just described. These web-applications show how to use and configure distinct logger hierarchies such that each web-application lives in its own independent logging universe. You will find deployment-ready war files *hello.war* and *tata.war* in the respective directories of each web-application. After deployment, you can access them as

   http://hostname:port/hello/hello.html

   http://hostname:port/tata/index.html

You should see log output appearing in the file */hello.log* for the *Hello* web-application and under */tata.log* for the *Tata* web-application as each web-application uses its own distinct logger hierarchy. Both applications have been tested under Tomcat 3.2.1, Tomcat 4.0.3 and Tomcat 4.1.12 but should work on any servlet container compatible with the Servlet API specification version 2.2 or later.

The two web-applications are extremely similar and differ almost exclusively by their name. Consequently, we will only list the salient parts of the *Hello* web-application.

Example 8-6: An initialization servlet (examples/chapter8/multipleHierarchies/Hello/-src/java/wombat/Log4jInit.java)

```
package wombat;
import org.apache.log4j.*;
import org.apache.log4j.spi.RootCategory;
import javax.servlet.http.*;
import javax.servlet.*;

public class Log4jInit extends HttpServlet {

  public void init() {
    ServletContext context =
                    getServletConfig().getServletContext();

    Hierarchy hierarchy =
              new Hierarchy(new RootCategory(Level.DEBUG));

    context.setAttribute("hierarchy", hierarchy);
```

```
   String prefix = getServletContext().getRealPath("/");
   String file = getInitParameter("log4j-init-file");
   // if the log4j-init-file is not set, then no point
   // in trying
   if(file != null) {
     new PropertyConfigurator().doConfigure(prefix+file,
                                           hierarchy);
     Logger logger =
             hierarchy.getLogger(Log4jInit.class.getName());
     logger.info("Logging initialized for Hello.");
   }
 }

 public void doGet(HttpServletRequest req,
                   HttpServletResponse res) {
   // nothing to do
 }
}
```

To create a new Hierarchy, it is enough to invoke its constructor by passing it a new RootCategory as argument. After creating a new hierarchy instance, the init() method configures it using a PropertyConfigurator. The doConfigure methods of all configurators admit a LoggerRepository as an argument, such that the instructions given within a configuration files apply to the supplied LoggerRepository instance. Here is the relevant code from Log4jInit.

```
   String prefix =  getServletContext().getRealPath("/");
   String file = getInitParameter("log4j-init-file");
   // if the log4j-init-file is not set, then no point
   // in trying
   if(file != null) {
     new PropertyConfigurator().doConfigure(prefix+file,
                                           hierarchy);
     Logger logger =
             hierarchy.getLogger(Log4jInit.class.getName());
     logger.info("Logging initialized for Hello.");
   }
```

The log4j-init-file parameter is defined within the *web.xml* file of the web-application. Subsequently loaded servlets or JSP pages simply retrieve the hierarchy instance from the servlet context and use that to obtain the loggers they need, as illustrated by the HelloServlet example.

Example 8-7: An simple servlet using the hierarchy defined by Log4jInit (examples/chapter8/multipleHierarchies/Hello/src/java/wombat/HelloServlet.java)

```
package wombat;
import java.io.*;
import javax.servlet.*;
import javax.servlet.http.*;
import org.apache.log4j.*;

public class HelloServlet extends HttpServlet {

  private Logger logger; // instance variable

  public void init() throws ServletException {
    ServletContext context =
                     getServletConfig().getServletContext();
    Hierarchy hierarchy =
              (Hierarchy) context.getAttribute("hierarchy");

    if(hierarchy == null) {
      context.log("The Hello web-application is not properly "
                 + "intialized.");
    } else {
      logger = hierarchy.getLogger(HelloServlet.class.getName());
    }
  }

  public void doPost(HttpServletRequest request,
                     HttpServletResponse response)
                     throws ServletException, IOException {

    String name = request.getParameter("name");
    response.setContentType("text/html");
    PrintWriter out = response.getWriter();

    if(logger!=null) {
      // if defined, use the logger as any other logger
      logger.info("About to say hello to "+name);
    }
    out.println("<HTML><BODY>");
    out.println("<H2> Hello " + name + ". How are you?</H2>");
    out.println("</BODY></HTML>");
    out.close();
  }
}
```

Note that the hierarchy is obtained once and for all within the init() method of the servlet. The servlet container calls the init() method exactly once after instantiating the servlet to indicate that it is being put into service. Version 2.3 of the Servlet specification introduced the `ServletContextListener` interface which offers small advantages over an initialization servlet. However, the principle of configuring a fresh log4j hierarchy at initialization time remains the same.

Using multiple hierarchies works well with code designed to use them. However, it does not compose well with a library which uses log4j but is unaware of multiple hierarchies. In log4j 1.2, a powerful yet transparent API was introduced to manage logger creation and retrieval.

Third solution

In a nutshell, the third solution relies on the servlet container to keep track of the execution context and provide a different logging environment for each context. Put differently, the servlet container provides a separate hierarchy instance for each web-application. Each logger object that log4j creates is attached to a hierarchy. The `Hierarchy` class implements the `LoggerRepository` interface by arranging logger objects in a tree according to their name.

The `Logger.getLogger()` method is actually implemented as follows:

```
static public Logger getLogger(String name) {
  return LogManager.getLogger(name);
}
```

In other words, the `Logger` class simply calls the class static `getLogger` method in the `LogManager` class. The `LogManager` class acts as a facade to a sub-system that retrieves `Logger` instances of varying types held in context-dependent repositories. From the user's perspective, the `LogManager` allows us to vary `Logger` implementation depending on the circumstances. Moreover, it controls the logging repository (i.e. hierarchy) where loggers are held depending on the application context. The behavior of `LogManager` is determined by the `RepositorySelector` it uses.

The `LogManager.getLogger()` method is implemented as follows:

```
public static Logger getLogger(String name) {
  // Delegate the actual manufacturing of the logger to
  // the logger repository.
  return repositorySelector.getLoggerRepository().getLogger(name);
}
```

The `repositorySelector` variable is a private class static variable of type `RepositorySelector`. The `RepositorySelector` interface contains only one method: `getLoggerRepository`. The `RepositorySelector` interface is reproduced (in its entirety) below:

```
package org.apache.log4j.spi;

public interface RepositorySelector {
  public LoggerRepository getLoggerRepository();
}
```

By default, the class static `repositorySelector` variable of the `LogManager` class is set to a trivial `RepositorySelector` implementation which always returns the same logger repository implemented as a `Hierarchy`. This object is referred to as the *default hierarchy*. What a coincidence, no?

The `LogManager` class has a setter method, namely the `setRepositorySelector()` method, which can cause the `LogManager` class to use a different `RepositorySelector` implementation. A top-level application such as a servlet container or an application server can set a `RepositorySelector` which can track application contexts and return the appropriate logger repository. The actual algorithm for tracking application context is the responsibility of the `RepositorySelector` implementation.

Let us implement a context sensitive repository selector. Let us call it CRS, for Contextual Repository Selector. CRS, or Contextual Repository Selector, is such that depending on the current execution context, it returns a different `LoggerRepository` instance. But since the `getLoggerRepository()` method takes no parameters how can it know the current execution context? The answer to this question depends on the servlet container. In Apache Tomcat for example, each web-application has its own class loader and Tomcat sets the Thread Context Classloader, or TCL, to be the class loader of the currently executing web-application.

Under this assumption our CRS can return a `Hierarchy` instance depending on the TCL. Below is a possible implementation of the CRS nominally designed for Tomcat.

Example 8-8: Contextual Repository Selector or CRS (examples/chapter8/CRS.java)

```
package org.apache.tomcat.wombat;

import org.apache.log4j.spi.RepositorySelector;
import org.apache.log4j.spi.LoggerRepository;
import org.apache.log4j.spi.RootCategory;
import org.apache.log4j.Hierarchy;
```

```java
import org.apache.log4j.Level;
import java.util.Hashtable;

public class CRS implements RepositorySelector {

  // key: current thread's ContextClassLoader,
  // value: Hierarchy instance
  private Hashtable ht;

  public CRS() {
   ht = new Hashtable();
  }

  // the returned value is guaranteed to be non-null
  public LoggerRepository getLoggerRepository() {
    ClassLoader cl =
            Thread.currentThread().getContextClassLoader();
    Hierarchy hierarchy = (Hierarchy) ht.get(cl);

    if(hierarchy == null) {
      hierarchy = new Hierarchy(new RootCategory(Level.DEBUG));
      ht.put(cl, hierarchy);
    }
    return hierarchy;
  }

  /**
   * The Container should remove the entry when the
   * web-application is removed or restarted.
   */
  public void remove(ClassLoader cl) {
    ht.remove(cl);
  }
}
```

The servlet container will set the repository selector to a CRS instance when it starts up. This is as simple as calling:

```java
        Object guard = new Object();
        LogManager.setRepositorySelector(new CRS(), guard);
```

Thereafter, the repository selector can only be changed by supplying the guard. Those who do not know it cannot change the repository selector. Note that the CRS implementation is container specific; it is part of the container, not log4j.

JNDI variant I

A variant of the above solution relies on the structure of the JNDI name space. In J2EE environments, each web-application is guaranteed to have its own JNDI context relative to the `java:comp/env` context. In EJBs, each enterprise bean (but not each application) has its own context relative to the `java:comp/env` context.

For example, a web-application could configure its deployment descriptor by adding an `env-entry` specifying its logging context. As in,

```
<web-app>
  <description>
    The deployment descriptor for the web-application
  </description>
  . . . .

  <env-entry>
  <description>
     Sets logging context for the web-application
  </description>

  <env-entry-name>logging-context</env-entry-name>
    <env-entry-value>TigerLoggingContext</env-entry-value>
    <env-entry-type>java.lang.String</env-entry-type>
  </env-entry>


    . . . .
</web-app>
```

Once the `env-entry` is set, a repository selector can query the JNDI application context (the `java:comp/env` context) to look up the value of `logging-context`. The logging context of the web-application will depend on the value of `logging-context` environment entry.

Below is a simplified implementation of a JNDI-based repository selector.

```
package org.apache.X;
import org.apache.log4j.spi.RepositorySelector;
import org.apache.log4j.spi.LoggerRepository;
import org.apache.log4j.spi.RootCategory;
import org.apache.log4j.Hierarchy;
import org.apache.log4j.Level;
import java.util.Hashtable;

import javax.naming.InitialContext;
import javax.naming.Context;
```

```
import javax.naming.NameNotFoundException;
import javax.naming.NamingException;

/** JNDI based Repository selector */
public class JNDIRS implements RepositorySelector {

  // key: name of logging context,
  // value: Hierarchy instance
  private Hashtable ht;
  private Hierarchy defaultHierarchy;

  public JNDIRS() {
   ht = new Hashtable();
   defaultHierarchy = new Hierarchy(new RootCategory(Level.DEBUG));
  }

  // the returned value is guaranteed to be non-null
  public LoggerRepository getLoggerRepository() {
    String loggingContextName = null;

    try {
      Context ctx = new InitialContext();
      loggingContextName =
                  (String) ctx.lookup("java:comp/env/logging-context");
    } catch(NamingException ne) {
      // we can't log here
    }

    if(loggingContextName == null) {
      return defaultHierarchy;
    } else {
      Hierarchy h = (Hierarchy) ht.get(loggingContextName);
      if(h == null) {
        h = new Hierarchy(new RootCategory(Level.DEBUG));
        ht.put(loggingContextName, h);
      }
      return h;
    }
  }
}
```

JNDIRS is container *independent*. JNDIRS relies on a standard technology, namely JNDI. Servlet and EJB containers are obliged to support JNDI because the administrative resources of most J2EE applications depend on it. In other words, JNDIRS merely leverages existing infrastructure to provide separation of logging. Just as importantly, the JNDI space is shared by JSP, Servlets and EJBs belonging to the same application. JNDIRS will work under all application servers (e.g. JBoss, Weblogic, Websphere) or from within servlets containers (e.g. Jetty, Resin, Tomcat) and even when Servlet containers are embedded within application servers.

JNDI variant II

Costin Manolache, a fellow Apache developer, has observed that the previous solution allows a malevolent application to spoof the logging environment of another application by setting the same string value for the `java:comp/env/logging-context` environment entry.

In other words, JNDIRS solves the *voluntary* logging separation problem but not the *mandatory* separation problem.

A container can prevent spoofing by malevolent applications by prefixing the name of the repository by either the application name or host name (in case multiple hosts live under the same container). Thus, if a given application desires to have a separate unspoofable logger repository, it will ask the container to do so in its deployment descriptor.

Here is a pseudo-implementation:

```
public class JNDIRS2 implements RepositorySelector {

    ... same as JNDIRS

    public LoggerRepository getLoggerRepository() {
      ... same as JNDIRS

      if(loggingContextName == null) {
       return defaultHierarchy;
      } else {
       if(mandatory separation for this application) {
         String applicationName = getNameThroughContainerMagic();
         loggingContextName = applicationName + loggingContextName;
       }
       Hierarchy h = (Hierarchy) ht.get(loggingContextName);
       if(h == null) {
         h = new Hierarchy(new RootCategory(Level.DEBUG));
         ht.put(loggingContextName, h);
       }
       return h;
      }
    }
  }
}
```

Contrary to the previous case, JNDIRS2 requires support from the container.

Advantages of context-based repository selectors

One advantage of context-based repository selectors is that log4j users will continue to call `Logger.getLogger` method in their code as usual, but their web-applications will use different hierarchy instances, effectively separating logging per web-application. It does not matter if *log4j.jar* file is on the CLASSPATH, in *JAVA_HOME/jre/lib/ext/* or in the container's "common" class loader. Moreover, web-applications will no longer need to add *log4j.jar* to their *WEB-INF/lib* directory.

There is another extremely important advantage. By controlling the logger repository the servlet container can also safely control the `Logger` implementation returned by the repository. The particular `Logger` implementation returned by each `LoggerRepository` may possess different characteristics. It can

- impose stricter security, for example based on the JDK 1.2 security model,

- return a `NullLogger` implementation in case logging is disabled for a given web-application,

- transparently interact with the web-application's container specific logging settings.

These implementations result respectively in higher security, better performance and better control.

9

CHANGES

*Change is not made without inconvenience, even
from worse to better.*

—RICHARD HOOKER

Between log4j version 1.1.x and 1.2

Log4j version 1.2 introduced many changes. In most cases however, it can be considered as a drop in replacement for log4j version 1.1.x. This section discusses the changes and backward compatibility issues.

Logger replaces Category

The most important change in 1.2 is the replacement of the `Category` class with the `Logger` class. To preserve backward compatibility, the `Logger` class extends the `Category` class such that it is always possible to use a logger object where a category object is expected. *In addition, whenever log4j is asked to produce a Category object, it will instead produce a Logger object.* Log4j version1.2 will never produce pure `Category` objects. Methods that previously accepted `Category` objects will continue to accept them.

For example, the following are all legal and will work as expected.

```
// Deprecated forms:
Category cat = Category.getInstance("foo.bar")
Logger logger = Logger.getInstance("foo.bar")
Category cat = Logger.getLogger("foo.bar")

// Preferred form for retrieving loggers:
Logger logger = Logger.getLogger("foo.bar")
```

There is absolutely no need for new client code to use or refer to the `Category` class in newly written code. Please avoid referring to it or using it. It is important to note that the introduction of the `Logger` class is backward compatible. You can still use the older `Category` class in your existing code; just avoid it in new code.

You may contend that having `Logger` extend `Category` is unintuitive – particularly because the `Logger` class is almost empty and relies entirely on the `Category` class for its implementation. Don't be fooled by the appearances. The `Category` class will be eventually removed and most of its contents transferred to `Logger`.

Compatibility issues with Category sub-classes

For most users the introduction of the `Logger` class is fully backward compatible. However, if you have sub-classed the `Category` class, then you need to heed the following points.

- Sub-classes of `Category` must extend `org.apache.log4j.Logger` and not `org.apache.log4j.Category`.

- The `org.apache.log4j.spi.CategoryFactory` class has been removed. It has been replaced with the `org.apache.log4j.spi.Logger-Factory` class. Thus, your subclass' factory must be of type `LoggerFactory`.

- The `Category.getInstance(String, CategoryFactory)` method has been removed. You need to invoke the `LogManager.getLogger(String, LoggerFactory)` method to create loggers of your subclass type.

- In configuration scripts parsed by `PropertyConfigurator` the `log4j.categoryFactory` keyword has been replaced with `log4j.loggerFactory`.

As explained in the previous chapter, we strongly recommend against sub-classing `Logger` or `Category` classes to introduce new printing methods; you can use the general purpose `log` method instead.

Level replaces Priority

In a very similar fashion, the `Priority` class has been replaced by the `Level` class. `Level` extends `Priority`. Whenever log4j is asked to produce a `Priority` object, it will instead produce a `Level` object. The constants `Priority.FATAL`, `Priority.ERROR`, `Priority.WARN`, `Priority.INFO`, `Priority.DEBUG` are now of type `Level`. Furtunately, these change should be completely transparent to all log4j users.

The `Priority.getPriority()` family of methods returning `Priority`, have been replaced with the `Priority.getLevel()` family of methods returning a `Level` instance.

LogManager, RepositorySelector and LoggerRepository classes

In log4j 1.2, we introduced a powerful API to manage the creation and retrieval of loggers depending on application context. See Chapter 8 further details.

Hierarchy wide enabling/disabling

In the `Hierarchy` class the `disable` family of methods have been removed and replaced by `setThreshold` and `getThreshold` methods. This change is not backward compatible.

10

FREQUENTLY AJKED QUEJTIONJ

Only reason can convince us of those three fundamental truths without a recognition of which there can be no effective liberty: that what we believe is not necessarily true; that what we like is not necessarily good; and that all questions are open.

—CLIVE BELL, *Civilization*

Why do salmon die so soon after spawning?

—ROBERT M. SAPOLSKY, *Why Zebras don't get ulcers*

Q 10.1 What are the installation requirements for log4j?

Log4j is JDK 1.1 compatible. However, several components may require packages that ship with Java 2 such as JNDI, Swing or JMX.

Q 10.2 Is log4j thread safe?

Yes, log4j can be safely used in multi-threaded applications. In particular, when multiple threads call the same appender, their requests are synchronized within the `doAppend` method of `AppenderSkeleton` which is the super-class of all appenders in log4j. Other parts of log4j employ the appropriate concurrency primitives to ensure thread safety.

Q 10.3 Can multiple Java Virtual Machines log to the same file using log4j?

No, there is no way for log4j to coordinate the access for a system resource, for example a file, between multiple JVMs. This restriction originates in the standard Java I/O libraries. Ignoring it is likely to result in garbled or even a completely corrupt log files.

Q 10.4 Can multiple appenders running in the same JVM log to the same file?

The answer is no. For performance and other technical reasons, log4j does not perform any synchronization between appenders. Having multiple appenders in the *same* JVM logging to the same file is not much different from having multiple appenders in *different* JVMs logging to the same file. See also the answer to the preceding question.

Q 10.5 How is log4j different from the `java.util.logging` API introduced in JDK 1.4?

The two APIs are very similar. As a result of our campaign to influence and improve the JSR47 API, the final version of JSR47 resembles log4j very closely.

There are two critical differences between the APIs. First, JSR47 requires JDK 1.4 whereas log4j is compatible with JDK 1.1 and later. Second, log4j offers much more functionality. It supports a rich configuration language, at least a dozen appenders and layouts as well as many other useful features.

Q 10.6 Does `java.util.logging` API threaten the future of log4j?

No, it does not. Log4j enjoys a very large user community that continues to grow vigorously. The expectation is for the log4j developers to continue to innovate and further widen the gap that exists between log4j and `java.util.logging` API. Moreover, as an open source project, log4j has a track record of quickly fixing bugs and reacting to demands of the user community.

Q 10.7 Why was the `Category` class renamed as `Logger` and the `Priority` class to `Level`?

The renaming was done essentially because that is how JSR47 names things. It is beneficial to adopt JSR47 terminology because all those who know the `java.util.logging` package will quickly feel equally at home with log4j. Moreover, the change makes it easy for users to switch from log4j to `java.util.logging` and hopefully, more often than not, the other way around.

Q 10.8 How can one log to different files based on level?

Setting the **Threshold** property of any appender extending `AppenderSkeleton` (all log4j appenders extend this class) will filter out all log requests with a level lower than the value of the threshold property.

Refer to section "Setting the threshold of an Appender" on page 58 and the section entitled "Setting the threshold of an Appender (XML)" on page 75 for further information on this topic.

Q 10.9 What guarantees are there (if any) for binary compatibility between different versions of log4j?

That is a deep and tough question. The problem of binary compatibility is intrinsic to the nature of software development. Unlike in other engineering endeavors, software can be easily modified or enhanced. This apparent ease of change makes it very easy to break compatibility with previous versions of the software.

For a widely used library like log4j, the question of binary compatibility is singularly acute. It is not uncommon to see an application composed of several libraries each of which depends on log4j for its logging. If any two of these libraries depend on incompatible versions of log4j, the application may not run smoothly. In a library of the size and breadth of log4j, it is exceedingly difficult to preserve 100% backward compatibility between the oldest and newest versions. Nevertheless, changes that break binary compatibility are few and very limited in scope such that the number of affected users is minimal. One notable exception is the deprecation of the `Category` class. If you read between the lines, the javadocs promise that the `Category` class will be kept around until mid-2003. This does not necessarily mean that it will be removed after that date...

Our current policy forbids the removal of a deprecated field, method or class before the completion of two release cycles. In other words, a method deprecated in log4j 1.2 *cannot* be removed until version 1.5 is officially released, leaving library developers over two years to adapt to changes in log4j. This policy applies to log4j version 1.2 and later. In earlier versions, the completion of only *one* release cycle was required for the removal of a deprecated method.

Q 10.10 What are the configurable options for `WombatAppender`?

Log4j uses JavaBeans introspection to dynamically infer the options its components. Any setter method admitting a single parameter which is a Java language primitive type (e.g. int, long), or any of the corresponding wrapper classes (e.g. `Integer, Long`), a `String`, or a `org.apache.log4j.Level`, corresponds to an option. For example, given that the `FileAppender` class contains the methods `setAppend(boolean)`, `setBufferSize(int)` and `setFile(String)`, it follows that **Append, BufferSize** and **File** are all valid option names. Log4j can also deal with setter methods taking a parameter of type `org.apache.log4j.Level`. For example, given that the `AppenderSkeleton` class has `setThreshold(Level)` as a member method, **Threshold** is a valid option for all log4j appenders extending `AppenderSkeleton`. Thus, although `WombatAppender` may not have an official list of its options, it is easy to discover them by looking at the setter methods present in the `WombatAppender` class and its super-classes.

Q 10.11 Why doesn't log4j implement duplicate appender detection?

When a given appender is attached to a logger, say "x.y" and to an ancestor logger, say "x", then logging requests made to "x.y" will appear twice in the output of the appender. See also trouble shooting item T 11-2 on page 193.

Log4j does not implement duplicate appender detection because implementing such functionality may not be trivial. Moreover, inadvertently attaching an appender to multiple loggers is usually the symptom of a misunderstanding. By propagating the error in a way observable by the user, we induce her to learn about the appender additivity rule. In general and as a matter of principle, log4j shuns away from compensating for user errors with the aim of keeping the implementation simple and robust.

Q 10.12 It is often repeated that sub-classing the `Logger` class is strongly discouraged. Why is that?

The direct reasons for this are explained in Chapter 8 under the heading "Writing your own Logger class." Moreover, the actual implementation of the `Logger` class in use depends on the `LoggerRepository` in use in a given context, as determined by the `RepositorySelector`. For example, it is entirely possible for two web-applications to use different logger repositories (hierarchies) that return different `Logger` implementations in response to the invocation of their `getLogger()` method. The ability to impose the `Logger` implementation is the reserved privilege of Servlet container or EJB container developers, not casual users. Ignoring this restriction is likely to cause trouble in future versions of J2EE containers that closely integrate with log4j. For more details on the `RepositorySelector` see the section entitled "The Wider Picture" in Chapter 8.

Q 10.13 Why aren't there any `isWarnEnabled`, `isErrorEnabled` and `isFatalEnabled` methods in the `Logger` class similar to `isDebugEnabled` or `isInfoEnabled`?

Given that logging statements of WARN, ERROR and FATAL level are rare, the existence of `isWarnEnabled`, `isErrorEnabled` and `isFatalEnabled` cannot be justified by performance considerations. If you really must, you may use the generic `isEnabledFor` method instead.

Q 10.14 What is the correct capitalization for log4j?

Log4j should be spelled in all lower case, as in log4j, except if it occurs as the first word in a sentence, like in this sentence.

Q 10.15 Why on earth is there bird on the cover of this book?

The cover of this book pictures Dave or more formally NGMC 91, a dromaeosaur fossil discovered by a farmer in China's Liaoning Province in the winter of 2000. According to specialists, Dave was a young dromaeosaur specimen covered with feathers. Its discovery added considerable weight to the theory that birds are the living descendants of dinosaurs. Mark Norell narrates the captivating story of Dave in his article "The Proof Is in the Plumage" which is available online at:

http://www.amnh.org/naturalhistory/0701/0701_feature.html

By studying fossils scientists make fascinating discoveries on the evolution of life on our planet. In a similar vein, by studying log traces developers can test various hypotheses for application failures and identify problems – even long after the application ceases to run. Enamored with the analogy between fossils and log traces, I started hunting for an attractive fossil illustration. My search stopped as soon as I bumped into Mick Ellison's drawing, which is reproduced herein with permission. Note that a feather also happens to be the emblem of the Apache Software Foundation. ☺

11

TROUBLE SHOOTING GUIDE

London Bridge is broken down,
Broken down, broken down,
London Bridge is broken down,
My fair lady.

—HENRY CAREY

This chapter contains a list of commonly encountered problems when using log4j. Before reporting bugs make sure that you have made an honest effort to study existing documentation. Please also see Eric S. Raymond's essay on asking questions the smart way. The URL for the essay is *http://www.tuxedo.org/~esr/faqs/smart-questions.html*

T 11-1   Log4j tells me to initialize properly.

Logging output is written to a target device by using an appender. If no appenders are attached to a logger or to any of its ancestors, you will get the following message at the first logging attempt:

```
log4j:WARN No appenders could be found for logger (some.logger.name).
log4j:WARN Please initialize the log4j system properly.
```

Log4j does not have a default logging target. It is the user's responsibility to ensure that all loggers can inherit an appender. This can be easily achieved by attaching an appender to the root logger.

T 11-2   Duplicates in log4j output.

The reason for observing duplicates in log4j output is either due to having added the same appender multiple times to the same logger, typically to the root logger or having added the same appender to different loggers, ignoring the fact that appenders are inherited cumulatively.

Log4j does not eliminate appender duplicates. In other words, if you add the same appender to a logger *n* times, that appender will be invoked *n* times to append to its target.

A slightly different cause of trouble is adding different appenders all sharing the same underlying output target to a given logger. In the most common occurrence of this phenomenon, the `BasicConfigurator.configure()` method is invoked multiple times. Each time it is invoked, this method adds an appender with a `System.out` target to the root logger.

One other common mistake is to forget that appenders are inherited cumulatively from the hierarchy. For example, if you add an appender, say *A*, to the root logger, all other categories will inherit *A* as an appender. Thus, if you add *A* to a logger, say *L*, then an enabled statement for logger *L*, will print on *A* twice: once because *A* is attached to the root logger and once because it is attached to logger L.

T 11-3   Deadlocks occurring after the introduction of log statements into an application.

On numerous occasions users have complained about deadlocks after introducing log statements into their code. However, without exception the bug was always in the application code not in log4j. This is not to say that log4j is totally bug-free but you need to provide some proof before accusing log4j and jumping to conclusions.

In the typical case, the introduction of logging statements reveals existing concurrency problems because log statements add delay which may change the order of execution among threads, causing an existing concurrency problem to come to surface.

T 11-4   Caller location information is printed as a "?" character.

Location information is extracted automatically by the `PatternLayout` conversion patterns %C, %F, %M and %L. However, some just-in-time (JIT) compilers make it impossible to extract location information. It is also possible that the compiler that generated the byte code may have omitted the line number table as is done by -O option of *javac* and *jikes* compilers.

You can remedy this problem by disabling the JIT compiler and by compiling the code without the -O option.

Wrappers or subclasses of the `Logger` class constitute a special case.

Wrappers or subclasses of `Logger` need to supply their fully qualified class name (FQCN) to the `Logger.log` method or to `Logger.forcedLog` methods so that the caller's location can be correctly extracted.

This approach will work perfectly well in all cases except a very rare and convoluted case, that is, if the class invoking the extended logger instance has the same prefix as the extended logger class. For example, calling a logger of type `com.foo.BarLogger` from the class `com.foo.BarLoggerTest` will not yield the correct caller information. To circumvent this rare problem, either rename the `com.foo.BarLoggerTest` class, or alternatively add a dot to the fully qualified name of the extending class that you supply to the `Logger.log` method. For the "com.foo.BarLogger" example, supply the string "com.foo.BarLogger." Note the dot suffix. If you fail to understand this paragraph, do not worry. The problem is rare, localized and otherwise harmless.

T 11-5 log4j:ERROR A "XYZAppender" object is not assignable to a "org.apache.log4j.Appender" variable.

This error occurs when log4j classes are loaded into memory by two distinct class loaders. According to section 4.3.4 of the Java Language Specification, when the same class is loaded by different class loaders, the resulting runtime copies are considered incompatible.

While processing configuration scripts log4j configurators often load classes into memory. Log4j is programmed such that configurators will first attempt load a required class using the thread context class loader (TCL) and if that fails, attempt to load the class using the current[27] class loader. Thus, log4j configurators will fail to load appenders or other log4j components when the thread context class loader has a different copy of log4j classes than the copy loaded by the current class loader. For example, assuming class loaders A and B both load a copy of log4j classes and the TCL is set to point to B, then invoking the `configure` method of a `DOMConfigurator` instance loaded by class loader A will cause an error. Indeed, the method responsible for loading the appender into memory will check that the class of the appender is assignable to `org.apache.log4j.Appender`. The check is done against the `org.apache.log4j.Appender` class loaded by A but since log4j gives preference to loading classes through the thread context class loader, B in this case, the Java runtime will consider the new appender (loaded by B) incompatible with the copy of `org.apache.log4j.Appender` class loaded by A.

---

[27] The current class loader is defined to be the class loader that loaded the currently executing object.

To get around this problem it suffices to make sure that only one and only one copy of *log4j.jar* is available to the class loader hierarchy of your application. This is not always possible because certain servlet containers and EJB containers use log4j internally for their own logging. These containers usually ship with a copy of *log4j.jar* which is visible by certain parts of their class loader hierarchy. However, when users deploy *log4j.jar* within their web-applications or ear files, depending on the delegation model of the application-specific class loaders, as well as the TCL settings, conflicts can arise. Tracking these conflicts requires good understanding of the class loader hierarchy of the container as well as precise details about the deployment of jar files at user's premises. It is not always possible to obtain accurate and timely information on these matters.

When all attempts to resolve the aforementioned problem fail despite your best efforts, then you can set the "**log4j.ignoreTCL**" system property as a last ditch solution[28]. When this system property is set to any value other than "false," log4j's class loading algorithm will ignore the value of the thread context loader and will only use the current class loader in order to locate and load classes. Note that the "**log4j.ignoreTCL**" property is only available in log4j version 1.2.6 and later. It is a system property that cannot be specified within configuration files.

T 11-6   `ClassCastException` when instantiating `Logger` sub-classes.

This exception is thrown because log4j does not support homonyms. For example, the following will systematically throw a `ClassCastException`

```
Logger c1 = Logger.getLogger("bad");
MyLogger c2 = (MyLogger) MyLogger.getLogger("bad");
```

where `MyLogger` is a subclass of `Logger`. The problem occurs because the second `getLogger` invocation will retrieve the logger created in the fist invocation. This instance is a `Logger` object and cannot be cast as `MyLogger`. Chapter 8 discusses the requirements for correctly sub-classing the `Logger` class.

T 11-7   log4j:WARN No such property [xyz] in some appender or layout

If during log4j configuration you get a warning about a nonexistent property, then you have probably misspelled a property or entered a truly unrecognized property for the component you are trying to configure.

---

[28] Up until the time of this writing, setting the "**log4j.ignoreTCL**" has always been successful in solving class loader problems.

Log4j version 1.0 did not complain about unrecognized properties whereas log4j versions 1.1 and later do complain.

T 11-8   I cannot log to Syslog under Linux.

If you are trying to log to the Unix Syslog under Linux using the `SyslogAppender`, then the Linux Syslog daemon must be configured to accept log input from the network. Otherwise, you will get an IOException: connection refused.

This can be done by adding the -r option when starting the daemon. Or more precisely:

- Login as the root user

- Edit file */etc/rc/init.d/syslog*

```
case "$1" in
start)
      echo -n "Starting system logger: "
      daemon syslogd -r
```

APACHE SOFTWARE LICENSE

This manual constitutes a separate body of work and is copyrighted by Ceki Gülcü and licensed to you under the terms of the license found at the beginning of this book. Nevertheless, given that it contains a small number of verbatim excerpts of log4j source code as well as parts of its documentation, the terms of the Apache Software License demand that this fact be acknowledged by reproducing the terms of the Apache Software License. Here it is:

```
/*
 * ====================================================================
 *                 The Apache Software License, Version 1.1
 * ====================================================================
 *
 * Copyright (C) 1999 The Apache Software Foundation. All rights
 * reserved.
 *
 * Redistribution and use in source and binary forms, with or without
 * modification, are permitted provided that the following
 * conditions are met:
 *
 * 1. Redistributions of source code must retain the above copyright
 *    notice, this list of conditions and the following disclaimer.
 *
 * 2. Redistributions in binary form must reproduce the above
 *    copyright notice, this list of conditions and the following
 *    disclaimer in the documentation and/or other materials provided
 *    with the distribution.
 *
 * 3. The end-user documentation included with the redistribution, if
 *    any, must include the following acknowledgment: "This product
 *    includes software developed by the Apache Software Foundation
 *    (http://www.apache.org/)."  Alternately, this acknowledgment may
 *    appear in the software itself, if and wherever such third-party
 *    acknowledgments normally appear.
 *
 * 4. The names "log4j" and "Apache Software Foundation" must not be
 *    used to endorse or promote products derived from this software
 *    without prior written permission. For written permission, please
 *    contact apache@apache.org.
 *
 * 5. Products derived from this software may not be called "Apache",
 *    nor may "Apache" appear in their name, without prior written
 *    permission of the Apache Software Foundation.
 *
 * THIS SOFTWARE IS PROVIDED ``AS IS'' AND ANY EXPRESSED OR IMPLIED
 * WARRANTIES, INCLUDING, BUT NOT LIMITED TO, THE IMPLIED WARRANTIES OF
 * MERCHANTABILITY AND FITNESS FOR A PARTICULAR PURPOSE ARE DISCLAIMED.
 * IN NO EVENT SHALL THE APACHE SOFTWARE FOUNDATION OR ITS CONTRIBUTORS
```

```
 *  BE LIABLE FOR ANY DIRECT, INDIRECT, INCIDENTAL, SPECIAL, EXEMPLARY,
 *  OR CONSEQUENTIAL DAMAGES (INCLUDING, BUT NOT LIMITED TO,
 *  PROCUREMENT OF SUBSTITUTE GOODS OR SERVICES; LOSS OF USE, DATA, OR
 *  PROFITS; OR BUSINESS INTERRUPTION) HOWEVER CAUSED AND ON ANY THEORY
 *  OF LIABILITY, WHETHER IN CONTRACT, STRICT LIABILITY, OR TORT
 *  (INCLUDING NEGLIGENCE OR OTHERWISE) ARISING IN ANY WAY OUT OF THE
 *  USE OF THIS SOFTWARE, EVEN IF ADVISED OF THE POSSIBILITY OF SUCH
 *  DAMAGE.
 *
 *  This software consists of voluntary contributions made by many
 *  individuals on behalf of the Apache Software Foundation.  For more
 *  information on the Apache Software Foundation, please see
 *  <http://www.apache.org/>.
 *
 */
```

Moreover, per Article 4 of the Apache Software license, this work uses the name "log4j" with written permission from the Apache Software Foundation.

The Apache Software License remains faithful to the sprit to the BSD License. It does not set restrictive conditions on extensions or redistributions, be they commercial or open-source. This liberal attitude has greatly facilitated the adoption of software from Apache.

For more information on the Apache Software Foundation please visit *http://www.apache.org/foundation/*. Most of the common queries about the Apache Software License are answered by Apache Software License FAQ, which is available at *http://www.apache.org/foundation/licence-FAQ.html*. Here is what the Apache Software License FAQ has to say on the Apache Software license.

What does it all mean?

Describing legal documents in non-legalese is fraught with potential for misinterpretation. Notwithstanding the text that follows, the actual text of the license itself is legally binding and authoritative.

That said, here is what the Apache license says in layman's terms:

It **allows** you to:

- freely download and use Apache software, in whole or in part, for personal, company internal, or commercial purposes;

- use Apache software in packages or distributions that you create.

It **forbids** you to:

- redistribute any piece of Apache-originated software without proper attribution;

- use any marks owned by The Apache Software Foundation in any way that might state or imply that the Foundation endorses your distribution;

- use any marks owned by The Apache Software Foundation in any way that might state or imply that you created the Apache software in question.

It **requires** you to:

- include a copy of the license in any redistribution you may make that includes Apache software;

- provide clear attribution to The Apache Software Foundation for any distributions that include Apache software.

It **does not require** you to:

- include the source of the Apache software itself, or of any modifications you may have made to it, in any redistribution you may assemble that includes it;

- submit changes that you make to the software back to the Apache Software Foundation (though such feedback *is* encouraged).

Appender

A destination for logging output.

Custom level

A level defined by the user.

java.util.logging API (JSR47)

The logging API introduced in JDK 1.4. It is the result of the JSR47 effort. See *http://jcp.org/aboutJava/communityprocess/review/jsr047/index.*html for more details.

Java System Property

Any of the string values available through the `getProperty`/`setProperty` methods in `java.lang.System`. You can set your java system properties with the -D option of the java tool, i.e. the launcher for Java technology applications.

For example,

```
java -Dlog4j.debug=true com.gopher.bar
```

will set the log4j.debug system property to true when launching the com.gopher.bar java application.

Layout

Layouts control the format of logging output. Some appenders delegate their formatting to a layout. A layout instance may be associated with at most one appender instance.

Location Information

The term "location information" designates the line number, file name and class name of the caller issuing a given log request. When possible, this information is automatically extracted by log4j.

Logger Printing Methods

The logger printing methods are `debug()`, `info()`, `warn()`, `error()`, `fatal()` and `log()` methods as defined in the `Logger` class.

INDEX